The New York Times

BEST OF THE WEEK SERIES: FRIDAY CROSSWORDS

THE NEW YORK TIMES BEST OF THE WEEK SERIES: FRIDAY CROSSWORDS.
Copyright © 2017 by The New York Times Company. All rights reserved.
Printed in China. For information, address St. Martin's Press,
175 Fifth Avenue, New York, NY 10010.

www.stmartins.com

All of the puzzles that appear in this work were originally published
in *The New York Times* from May 8, 2015, to November 11, 2016.
Copyright © 2015, 2016 by The New York Times Company.
All rights reserved. Reprinted by permission.

ISBN 978-1-250-13322-9

Our books may be purchased in bulk for promotional, educational, or business use.
Please contact your local bookseller or the Macmillan Corporate and Premium Sales Department
at 1-800-221-7945, extension 5442, or by e-mail at MacmillanSpecialMarkets@macmillan.com.

First Edition: May 2017

11   10   9   8   7

The New York Times

BEST OF THE WEEK SERIES: FRIDAY CROSSWORDS
50 Challenging Puzzles

Edited by Will Shortz

ST. MARTIN'S GRIFFIN ☙ NEW YORK

The New York Times

SMART PUZZLES
Presented with Style

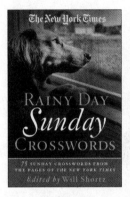 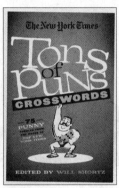  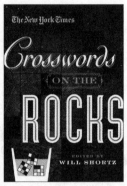 

   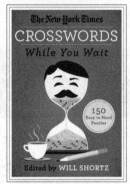 

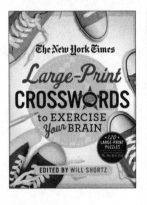  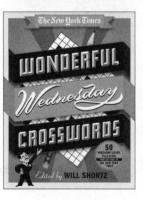 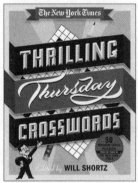 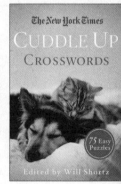

Available at your local bookstore or online at www.nytimes.com/nytstore

✠ St. Martin's Griffin

f fbmacmillan.com/smp/willshortz

ACROSS

1 Prominent feature of dubstep music
5 Try to avoid an accident, maybe
11 Fields of food?
14 Mass observance
15 Lit from above?
16 It sounds like you
17 Boss
19 Big source of coal: Abbr.
20 Song that Paul McCartney wrote at 16
22 Generic
23 Street __
24 Goddess who caused the Trojan women to riot in the "Aeneid"
25 Parting chorus
31 Sinner's heart?
32 Having a protective cover, of a sort
33 One side of the Mideast
34 Wear for a flower child
35 Something you may need to get off your chest
38 Provocative performance
39 Create an icicle, say
40 Heart's partner
41 Mets' division, for short
43 Stance
49 Bordeaux toasting time
50 Ketchup base
51 Stretch out
52 "Ave Maria," e.g.
53 "Sure, I'm game"
54 Rock's __ Soundsystem
55 Worked (out)
56 Binding exchange

DOWN

1 Base for some ice cream
2 Stadium noisemaker
3 First bishop of Paris
4 Perceived to be
5 Embarrassed
6 They take place in theaters
7 "The Time Machine" people
8 Sauce thickener
9 Scream one's head off
10 Start to go down the drain
11 2009 million-selling Justin Bieber release
12 Some vaudeville fare
13 Grassy surface
18 Edge
21 Symbol on a cello or tuba composition
26 Slide presentation?
27 Mature
28 Historic computer
29 Famed cabin site
30 Flight figures, for short
32 Start of a Saturday night catchphrase
33 Big cheese wheels?
34 "Walk on the Wild Side" singer, 1973
35 Like Swiss steak
36 Creamy, whitish dish
37 Relevance
38 Beautifully worded
39 Alaska's __ Park Road
40 Brief period
42 Edge
44 Texter's "Alternatively . . ."
45 Gumshoe Charles
46 "Lucky Jim" author
47 Tie securely
48 Winnebago relative

by David Steinberg

2

ACROSS

1 Hit 1981 Broadway musical made into a 2006 film
11 Like five-star accommodations
15 Pet project for a 14-Down
16 Regarding
17 Acts in some rituals
18 Deal with a huge catch
19 One-named New Ager
20 One who might say "Brace yourself!," in brief?
21 "Don't ___!" (parental admonition)
22 Mag crowning a "Bachelor of the Year"
24 Plot element?
25 Bogus, to Brits
27 What Indiana University's superimposed "I" and "U" looks like
28 Sioux City-to-Fort Collins dir.
29 Place
30 Bounty work?
33 Scare
35 Treaty of Rome creation, for short
36 Find x, say
37 Aid in collecting evidence
40 It forms part of the Polish/German border
41 Burgundy season
42 Professional fixer
43 Hawkeye rival, briefly
45 Cheesemaking need
47 ___ Brava, Spain
48 Old Peloponnesian power
49 Label a bomb
50 "I'm at your disposal"
54 Slender
55 Desk accessory
57 Geological units
58 Make one's head spin?
59 Bit at the bottom
60 Hit 2005 Broadway musical made into a 2014 film

DOWN

1 Time to strike
2 First name in gossip
3 ___ Krenz, last Communist leader of East Germany
4 "Henry V" battle setting
5 Boris or Natasha, to Fearless Leader
6 Contract
7 Statement after a valiant attempt
8 Common concerto closer
9 Stock to be split?
10 Ceremonially gowned grp.
11 Meal, in Italy
12 Who wrote "There is no sin except stupidity"
13 Goes from the top
14 One with a lot to think about
21 23-Down travelers
23 See 21-Down
24 Old geographical inits.
25 Possibility considered after an air accident
26 Combustion contraption
27 Noted kidnappee of 1613
29 Slashed
31 Put in stitches
32 Guessed
34 Romeo's repertoire
38 What a birdie flies over
39 Take all the dishes from
44 Solid
46 Request to leave out for takeout?
47 Bring all the dishes to
49 Father of the mariée
51 Cosmetician Laszlo
52 Gray of R&B
53 Things opened in the morning
55 "All the way with ___" ('64 slogan)
56 Scratch

by Peter A. Collins

ACROSS

1 Little man
5 Less likely to be caught
15 Dueler's option
16 Washington city famous for its sweet onions
17 Virginia and Truckee Railroad terminus
18 Grave words
19 Keeps from backing up
21 Disappointed outburst
22 Spring's opposite
23 Number of letters
27 Women who might share the same surname
30 Net game?
31 Pet sound
34 Administrative title
35 Man in black, perhaps
36 Novelist Jaffe
37 Dimwit
38 Rule of order?
40 Lincoln signed it into law in 1862
41 Like some deliveries
43 "I forbid," to Caesar
44 ___ Sea (the "Sea of Islands")
45 Collections of episodes
48 Cab supplier
53 Part of a pod
54 Chlorofluorocarbons damage it
55 Vassal's reward
56 Shot blockers
57 Lose vividness

DOWN

1 Major quinoa exporter
2 Boot hills?
3 Carol king
4 Taxonomic terms, for instance
5 Big gulp
6 Tropical acquisitions, maybe
7 Classic vineyard tree
8 Cask beverage
9 Fly the coop
10 Smallest prime
11 School attended by Churchill
12 Old war story
13 Give a lift to
14 Merlin Olsen's team
20 Pro-am tourney, often
23 "Der Judenstaat" movement
24 Laser alternative
25 What parents might prompt kids to say
26 Exec's perk
27 Tom Collins ingredient
28 Handle again?
29 Eight-footer?
31 Suspensions of activity
32 Nestled
33 Steam engine pioneer James
36 Leaves, as in a western
38 Multiplicity
39 Broad bean
40 Mount St. ___
41 Won thing
42 Talked ad nauseam
44 Not on base?
45 Future reporter
46 Needs to make a retraction
47 On base
49 Dry, on Champagne bottles
50 "Rockaria!" band, briefly
51 Place to go, for short
52 Strong base

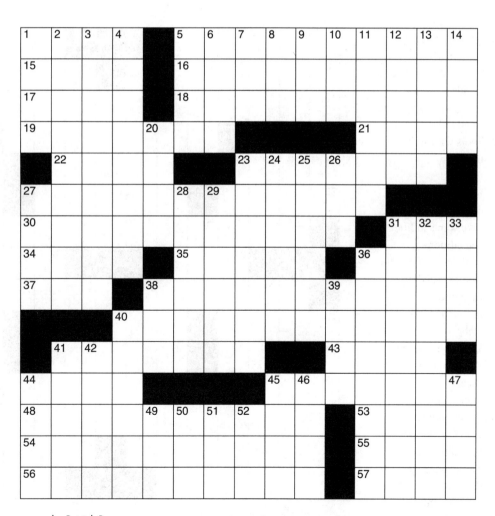

by Patrick Berry

4

ACROSS

1 Viking girl in "How to Train Your Dragon"
7 Intimates
13 Comics tyke
15 Starling of book and film
16 Epic number
18 So-called "fifth qtrs."
19 Postwar German nickname
20 Kenan's sitcom partner
21 Next
23 Irrelevant info
24 Trinidad o Tobago
25 Shot putters' needs?
26 Squash
27 Unleashes (on)
28 Its main characters go to hell
31 ___ Green, 2006 Bond girl
32 Chris who sang "The Road to Hell," 1989
33 Tools with swiveling blades
40 Directed
41 Fantasy sports option
42 Like some additions and editions
44 With 36-Down, bit of clothes mending
45 Like drafts
46 Emphatic type: Abbr.
47 Lance on a bench
48 Snowflake or crystal shape
50 Outer limit
51 Functioning again
54 Like Charlie Brown's kite, ultimately
55 Large game bass
56 Great-aunt in "David Copperfield"
57 Saws

DOWN

1 Dandy wear
2 Enveloped
3 Byzantine art bit
4 Pensioned: Abbr.
5 Light music source?
6 Appealing figure?
7 Rice elbows, e.g.
8 Facility
9 Lilt bit
10 Registers
11 Big name in car parts
12 Automotive models S and X
14 For three, to Frédéric
15 Chuck who advised Nixon
17 French-speaking land where John James Audubon was born
22 Fashion designer Lepore
24 Bar-Ilan University student, e.g.
29 Power inits. beginning in 1933
30 "An ___ held by the tail is not yet caught" (old proverb)
33 It's named for its five carbon atoms
34 Old sandlot game
35 Baroque
36 See 44-Across
37 Internet hookups?
38 Fairly clean, so to speak
39 Comic book writer with a National Medal of Arts
40 Winter wear resembling overalls
43 Graybeards
48 Boot
49 Add superfluous stuff to
52 Some chess pieces: Abbr.
53 Period of veinticuatro horas

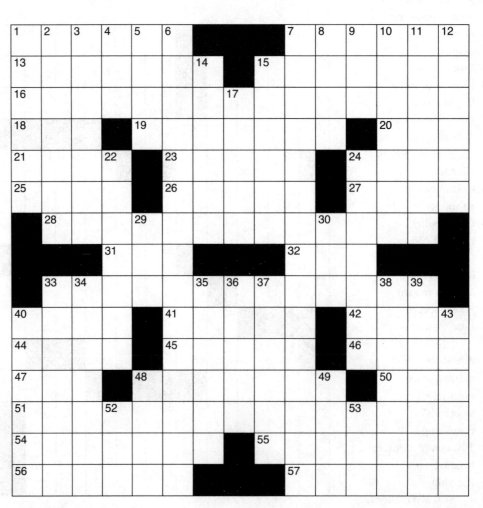

by Paula Gamache

ACROSS

1 Shout when there's no cause for alarm?
5 2008 R&B Grammy winner for "Growing Pains"
10 Throw
14 Little opening?
15 Peripheral
16 Like many flu sufferers
17 Taking some heat?
19 Heat meas. that also names a major L.A. TV station
20 Request at a ticket window
21 Really get to
22 Bit of vaquero gear
23 Product boasting "a unique blend of 23 flavors"
25 Dungeons & Dragons race
26 University of Cincinnati squad
27 Replies from con men?
28 Norman who wrote "A River Runs Through It"
29 Smidge
30 Resident
31 Ed promoter
34 Green-glazed Chinese porcelain
35 Attorney general under Bush 41
36 Not fit for Passover
38 "Miss Julie" composer
39 Like literati
40 Networking aid
41 Opposite of division
42 It's similar to pale lager
44 Going __
45 Possible purse pooches
46 Provide design details for
47 Comparatively corrupt
48 Send packing
49 "One World" musician John
50 Mancala playing piece
51 Fiddle (with)

DOWN

1 Full of sauce
2 The Ainapo Trail is on its slope
3 Rattled
4 Entrees from the frozen food department
5 Lisa of "The Cosby Show"
6 Selene's Roman counterpart
7 Relative of "Without a doubt" in a Magic 8 Ball
8 Powerful foe of the Man of Steel
9 Watt-second fraction
10 Battery container?
11 Come to terms with
12 They often follow showers
13 Shortest-serving U.S. vice president (31 days)
18 Interjection of dejection
21 Tart flavor
24 Primp
26 Vehicle that's loaded in a Harry Belafonte hit
28 Highlight for some hockey fans
30 For-profit university with dozens of U.S. campuses
31 What a reverse stock split increases
32 Like much of northern Siberia
33 Chair pair
34 Prestigious Pasadena institution
35 A rut often leads to it
36 Delaware Valley tribe
37 Groups of power brokers
38 Change
39 Oktoberfest fare
40 Embarrassing sound in a lecture hall
43 Start for seas or seasons
45 Atlanta-based media inits.

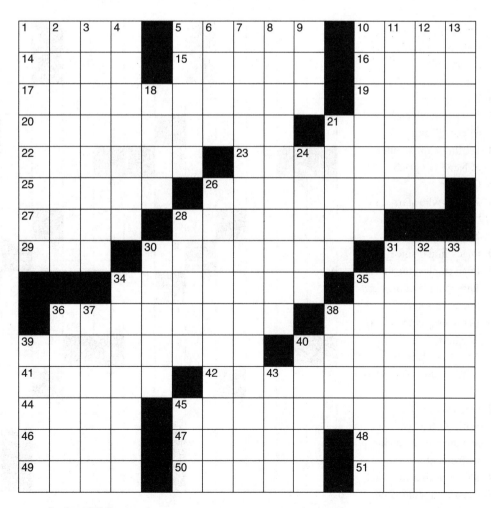

by David Phillips

6

ACROSS

1 Stare in astonishment
5 Horatian or Keatsian
9 Clean freak of sitcomdom
14 Long
15 Dance that might give you a lift?
16 Campbell on a catwalk
17 Setting for fans
20 Fortune 100 company whose name starts with a silent letter
21 Part of le Parlement français
22 Judgmental sound
23 Chicago exchange, in brief
25 First name on a B-29
27 Jonathan Swift satire
33 Dent or crack
34 Frank narrative
35 Balloon-carried probe
36 Prior: Abbr.
38 Circumvent
40 Zip
41 System in which 33 and 63 are "!" and "?"
43 Southern alma mater of Newt Gingrich
45 Category
46 Actress who starred in "The Fault in Our Stars," 2014
49 Snack brand since 1967
50 Luau staples, for short
51 Threepio's first master
53 Some cat sounds?
56 Certain absentee voter, for short
59 2012 Best Actress nominee for "Zero Dark Thirty"
62 Opposite of afore
63 With 67-Across, attachment to a string instrument
64 Shade similar to camel
65 Classic car company co-founder
66 City on der Rhein
67 See 63-Across

DOWN

1 Mad
2 Plot piece
3 Question upon completing an argument
4 Like many farm animals
5 Sister brand of Alpha-Bits
6 Sleuths connect them
7 "Of wrath," in a hymn title
8 John Steinbeck novel
9 De-clogs
10 Shetlands turndown
11 Crawl
12 They might work at a revival, for short
13 Chance
18 Took a 13-Down
19 "Hawaii Five-O" nickname
24 Collectors of DNA, prints, etc.
26 Avian symbol of Ontario
27 Grp. behind the Oscars
28 Reed section?
29 Nonplussed
30 Amazon offering
31 Nonplus
32 Unsafe, as a boat
37 Number on a grandfather clock
39 Drop __
42 "It's probably a trick, but tell me"
44 They join teams
47 Wire transfer?: Abbr.
48 Role for which Michael C. Hall got five straight Emmy nominations
51 Cracked
52 Mount near the Dead Sea
54 37-Down, to Diego
55 Doctor seen by millions
57 Hauteur
58 Hardware bit
60 U.S. Army E-7
61 "__ Vickers," Sinclair Lewis novel

by Mary Lou Guizzo

ACROSS

1 One inclined to patronize a farmer's market
9 Cetacean's closest relative
14 Ready for a road trip, say
15 Old epic recounting wanderings
16 Ones who don't take a seat?
17 With precision
18 Reply of feigned surprise
19 It leads to early advancement
20 Bombshell
21 Longtime Princess Royal
23 Bega with the hit "Mambo No. 5"
24 "Wrath of the Titans" antagonist
25 Region around a star "just right" for habitable planets
30 Like some jet refuelings
31 "Sometimes a Great Notion" novelist, 1964
32 Puerto Rico is on it year-round, for short
35 Little bit
36 Subject of a museum in Louisville, Ky.
38 24/7/365 facilities
39 Alternative to chinos
41 Moving like 43-Down
44 Have a bawl
48 Words of confidence
49 "I knew a man Bojangles and __ dance for you . . ." (1968 song lyric)
50 They're not refined
52 Naval hero with five U.S. counties named for him
54 Asset in climbing the corp. ladder
57 Big __
58 Means of getting the word out?
59 When many fans come out
61 Beverage brand with three leaves in its logo
62 Used car selling point
63 Long hoops shots
64 Presenter of many listicles

DOWN

1 A baby one is called a cria
2 Major Taiwanese export
3 House of cards?
4 Bother
5 Hop, skip or jump
6 Jazz singer whose surname came from pig Latin
7 Tolkien character
8 They're longer than singles, briefly
9 Give attention
10 Flabbergasted
11 Appropriately named Reds legend
12 Brew named for a Czech city
13 Long, trying trips
15 Aimée of film
20 "Knock yourself out"
22 Cabinetry material
23 Rule, in Rennes
26 Possible response to "Huh-uh!"
27 Mount with the Cave of Zeus
28 September honoree
29 Potato __
32 The discovery of penicillin, e.g.
33 Casting director?
34 Act the judge
37 Cover for someone, say
40 Bourbons, e.g.
42 Time magazine's "scholarly Everest," for short
43 Oil or honey
45 2009 and '13 sci-fi role for Zoë Saldana
46 Refined
47 Boob tube
51 Bergen dummy
53 Butt end?
54 Where to look for starters
55 "Love Is Just a Four-Letter Word" singer
56 Complete
59 Play __ (be disruptive)
60 Conservation org. with a panda logo

by Brandon Hensley

8

ACROSS

1 Order
5 ___ palm
9 It's made with syrup
13 Town near Ireland's Shannon Airport
15 A caller may be on this
16 Track type
17 & 18 Italian-born composer
19 Something a scow lacks
20 It's often hooked
21 Carlos the Jackal, for one
23 Start of a Beatles refrain
25 Eastern titles
26 ___ loss
27 Bars in cars
29 "A ___ champion never handled sword": "Henry VI, Part I"
31 "Understood"
33 Danny's love in "Ocean's Eleven"
34 & 35 German-born composer
38 Man's name that spells a fruit backward
41 Class lists?
44 Takes one's sweet time
48 Kind of car or class
50 2014 Oscar winner for Best Foreign Language Film
51 Space cadet's need?
53 Prompt
54 His first tweet ended "I bless all of you from my heart"
57 What the lowing herd wind slowly o'er, in verse
58 For the calorie-conscious
59 & 60 Austrian-born composer
61 N.B.A. coach Spoelstra
62 Put on
63 Spiny shrub
64 Without
65 Ligurian Sea feeder
66 North Sea feeder

DOWN

1 "Austin Powers" villain
2 Out of this world?
3 Longtime grandmotherly "General Hospital" actress
4 Short-beaked bird
5 "Aren't you forgetting something?"
6 Jumble behind a computer desk
7 Hazel relatives
8 "Cool, man!"
9 Popular 9-Across
10 Gorged
11 Shakespeare character who says "I dare damnation"
12 Paying close attention
14 Retirement party, e.g.
18 Without
22 Tour grp.
24 "Happy Days" malt shop owner
28 File certain papers
30 "View From the U.N." memoirist
32 Hosp. staffers
35 Cry that's often doubled
36 Place for a bust
37 Doubling up?
38 Food
39 Port alternative
40 "Sign me up!"
42 Heating equipment
43 Put completely (in)
45 TV option, for short
46 Engineer Gray who co-founded Western Electric
47 Aid
49 Shepard's role in "The Right Stuff"
52 ___ Allen Express (Amtrak train in the Northeast)
55 Horror movie sounds
56 Letter ender
60 "Whew!"

by Jacob Stulberg

ACROSS

1 1991 Scorsese/De Niro collaboration
9 Something exciting to play with
15 Fragile fabric made from certain plant fibers
16 Tough leather
17 Amscrayed
18 One getting lots of take-out orders?
19 Edward VII or VIII, in India: Abbr.
20 ___ nullius (no one's property)
21 Pioneering labor leader Samuel
22 Was suddenly successful
24 Nullius ___ (of no legal force)
25 Like NSFW links
26 Kennedy and Bush 41, but no other U.S. presidents
28 Chuck
29 "Mum's the word"
31 Little, in Lockerbie
32 Cross collections, e.g.
33 Roughneck's workplace
35 It's in the far northwest
37 Product of Greek culture?
38 Moderately dry
39 True
40 Splitting words
41 "Mr. ___" (Styx hit)
42 Blow hole?
45 Winner's prize on "RuPaul's Drag U"
46 Gap fillers, of sorts
47 "My response was . . . ," informally
48 "Grey's Anatomy" actress with five straight Emmy nominations
50 Hands on deck
51 Hand wringer's cry
52 Flip
53 Bridge tolls, e.g.

DOWN

1 They might spook spelunkers
2 Where the San Antonio Spurs used to play
3 Blowhard
4 Job ad inits.
5 Broccoli bit
6 Like pain after treatment, often
7 Nails
8 Stop sign?
9 Unwanted attention
10 Checks out
11 Adds with a whisk
12 Makeshift coaster, maybe
13 Reason to hold your nose
14 Gen ___ (millennials)
21 Yellow-flowered plant producing a sticky resin
23 Chicago Fire's sports org.
24 Noisy recreation vehicles
26 Blanket
27 "Uh-huh, I believe THAT"
29 "Hold your horses"
30 Forgo a night out
32 His wife and sons were Depression-era criminals
34 Couple taken out on a rainy day
36 2/2, to Toscanini
37 Key-ring ornament
39 Demolition cleanup machine
41 ___ Barber, five-time Pro Bowler from the Tampa Bay Buccaneers
42 Like some legal decrees
43 Owl's hoot, to some
44 Pomeranian, e.g.
45 Cross words
48 Trifle
49 Org. in the gulf war's Operation Granby

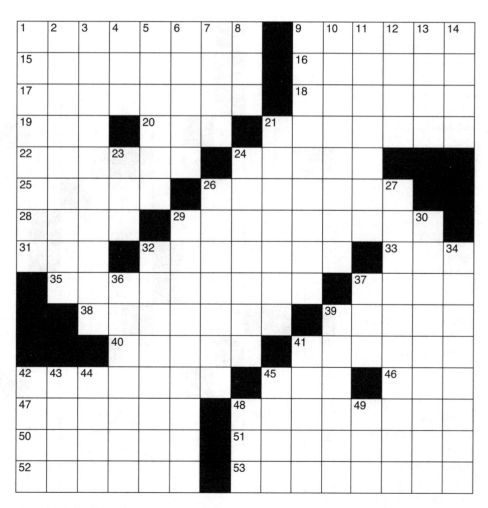

by Paula Gamache

10

ACROSS

1 King or queen
4 Record six-time N.B.A. M.V.P.
15 Northeast sch. in the Liberty League
16 Rather caricatured
17 Understanding responses
18 One involved in a pyramid scheme?
19 Broke down, say
21 End of a Hemingway title
22 Fleck on the banjo
23 Atlanta train system
25 Drink often served chilled
27 Bert's sister in children's literature
28 Dandy headpieces
31 Catch
33 Excessively harsh
35 Philadelphia train system
39 Trio in Greek myth
40 New Deal org.
41 Pope John Paul II's first name
42 Was out
43 Aida in "Aida," e.g.
45 Go preceder
47 Unsightly spots
48 Country music's ___ Brown Band
51 Digs
53 Early customer of Boeing
54 Old Testament kingdom
56 Like the cities Yazd and Shiraz
59 Transport method usually used in the winter
61 One who can see right through you?
64 Author Chinua Achebe, by birth
65 Back-to-back hits
66 "Kate Plus 8" airer
67 Harmless slitherer
68 See 63-Down

DOWN

1 Something that's knitted
2 Here today, gone tomorrow
3 Quite different
4 Latin grammar case: Abbr.
5 Country with the King Hamad Highway
6 Trio abroad
7 Shoshone relatives
8 Player of Cleopatra in "Two Nights With Cleopatra"
9 Who had a #1 hit with "Toot Toot Tootsie (Goo'bye)"
10 Suffix with meth-
11 Spill everything
12 Politico with the 2007 autobiography "Promises to Keep"
13 "The Jungle Book" wolf
14 Put back on
20 Muscle used in bench-pressing
24 Simple dance
26 Things that may be blown
28 Some email pics
29 Photographic memory or perfect pitch, e.g.
30 Master
32 Cincinnati athlete
34 NASA part: Abbr.
36 Outlaws
37 Not too awful
38 Consumables often described with a percentage
44 Comic who said "I open my eyes, remember who I am, what I'm like, and I just go 'Ugh'"
46 Worker on London's Savile Row
48 Weightlessness
49 1943 Churchill conference site
50 Computer programmer
52 Dives
55 Useful thing to keep on hand?
57 "Janie's Got ___" (1989 Aerosmith hit)
58 First in a historical trio
60 Almond ___ (candy)
62 Be short
63 With 68-Across, end of a Hemingway title

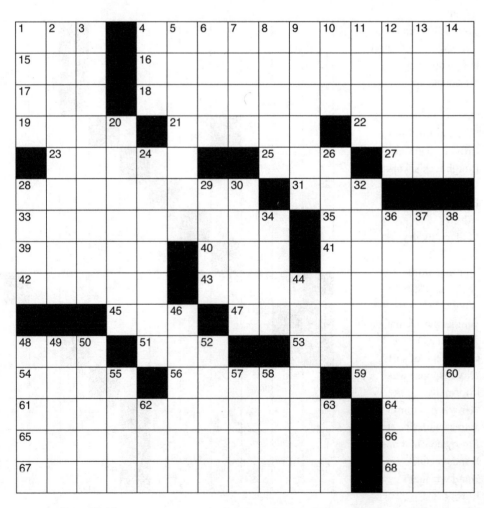

by Evans Clinchy

11

ACROSS

1 Phylicia of stage and screen
7 Reduce to tears?
15 Some highway conveniences
17 Unwelcome war report
18 French force
19 Back tracks?
20 ___-relief
21 Blood letters
22 Green org.?
25 Deem to be dumb
31 Quaint means of manipulation
32 Common instruments in jazz combos
33 Cyclist in peak condition?
34 Fine source of humor, with "the"?
35 This was once "art"
36 U.P.S. unit: Abbr.
37 It may come with a price to pay
40 Cousin of a frittata
44 Major tributary of the Missouri
46 Tamarack trees
50 Didn't stand firm in negotiations
51 "Fish Magic" artist
52 Get beaten by

DOWN

1 Aid for clean living
2 Hyundai luxury sedan
3 Blasts inboxes
4 Billionaire, for one
5 "___ sow . . ."
6 Award since W.W. I
7 Outcome in Eden
8 His: Fr.
9 Dressed
10 Glamour rival
11 Bad singers?

12 "Star Wars" saga nickname
13 Driver's aid
14 What makes a top stop?
16 Grammy-nominated blues guitarist in the Louisiana Music Hall of Fame
21 Husky cousins
22 Punt propeller, e.g.
23 Says, informally
24 ___ Toy Barn ("Toy Story 2" locale)
25 Alloy of tin and lead
26 Just slightly
27 Order to a sommelier, maybe

28 Bow out
29 Not out, but not necessarily up
30 Doctors
31 Debussy contemporary
32 1922 Physics Nobelist
33 1959 Kingston Trio hit
37 Explorer alternative
38 Star seeker?
39 Canvas primer
40 City northeast of Kiev
41 Head Stone
42 Biol. branch
43 The New Yorker film critic Anthony
44 +/−
45 Biol. and others

46 Concert piece
47 Kid's cry
48 College final?
49 It's sometimes shown in the corner of a TV screen, for short

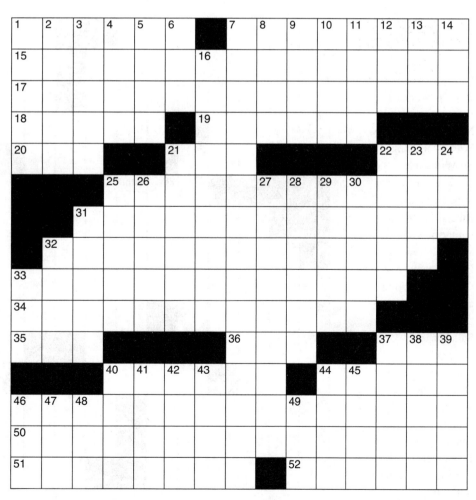

by Martin Ashwood-Smith

ACROSS

1 Subcompact
8 Subject to an air attack
14 Well-known, now
16 Big name in guitars
17 Put on a pedestal
18 Lock horns
19 Fall foliage color
20 "Girl With a Hoop" painter
22 Banff wildlife
23 First name in cosmetics
25 Common waiting room viewing
26 Fictional race of the distant future
27 Picasso masterpiece with a French title
30 Cousin of a blintz
31 "Hotel Impossible" airer
34 P.M. who won the 1957 Nobel Peace Prize
35 Miraculous solutions
36 Friends, in slang
37 Sir William ___, so-called "Father of Modern Medicine"
38 Runs off at the mouth
39 Guitar-making wood
40 Post-tragedy comment
45 Common question after a name is dropped
46 Salad base
49 ___ war
50 Like some warfare
52 Decision debated for decades
54 Worrisome engine sound
55 Fret about
56 Corsairs and Rangers of the 1950s
57 Things in keys

DOWN

1 Op art pattern
2 It flows for nearly 2,000 miles in Asia
3 Big mushroom producer, in brief
4 "___ war": F.D.R.
5 Frame from a drawer
6 "Jake and ___" (comedy web series)
7 Give a dynamite finish?
8 Form of civil disobedience
9 It's a lift
10 Bled
11 Kings' supporters
12 Dropped like a jaw
13 Book before Daniel
15 Office drones
21 Amoeba feature
24 Gives a lift
26 Lubitsch of old Hollywood
28 State
29 Denoting the style in which one might consider this clue to be written
30 Sympathetic sorts
31 Gets from A to B instantly
32 Says one can make it, say
33 Well
34 Be in store
35 Means of obtaining private information
39 Name in many van Gogh titles
41 "Incredible!"
42 Italian wine
43 Guitar-making wood
44 Ones preparing Easter eggs
46 Presumption
47 "___ problem"
48 In public
51 Ending with Manhattan
53 Bugs on the road

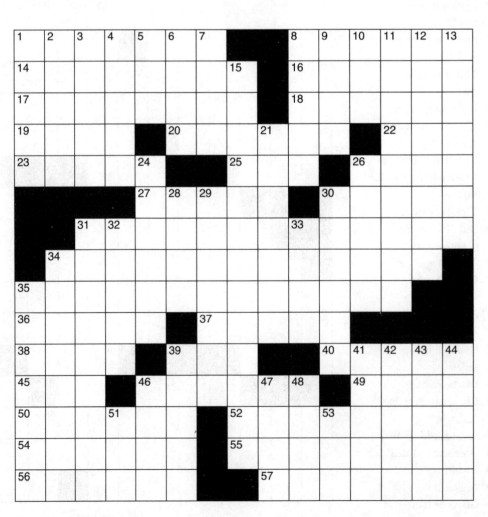

by Michael Wiesenberg

ACROSS

1 Far and away one's favorite writer?
7 Mellow R&B track
14 Fly
15 Primitive and backward
16 Items with decorative scrolls
17 Slice from a book?
18 Pay homage, in a way
19 "___ off!" (phrase of homage)
20 Scratches (out)
21 French border region
23 One on the trail, for short
24 Room in Clue
27 20-20 and others
28 Bungling
31 There's one for Best New American Play
32 Extreme
34 500-pound bird hunted to extinction
35 Film character who said "Look, I ain't in this for your revolution, and I'm not in it for you, Princess"
37 A, B or C, but not X, Y or Z
39 ___ caution
40 Knee jerk, e.g.
42 Head shop buy
43 Unite
45 Hue
46 "Woe ___ them that call evil good": Isaiah
47 "The Lost Tapes" rapper
48 Took care of, as guests
50 Z's : sleep :: wavy lines : ___
52 ___ Préval, twice-elected president of Haiti
53 Crude Halloween costume
57 "Drink" for the overly critical
59 Crèche setting
60 Schiller work set to music by Beethoven
61 Little rock
62 Symbol of modern communication
63 Out of retirement?

DOWN

1 Stuff
2 Flush
3 Water source for 11 countries
4 Some blonds
5 Snorkeling mecca
6 ___ Echos (French daily)
7 Pink property
8 Cuts (off)
9 Light air, on the Beaufort scale
10 "It's our time to go!"
11 "Glengarry Glen Ross" co-star, 1992
12 Chill in bed?
13 Pro team with blue-and-orange jerseys
15 Orthodontic device
19 Supposed morning remedy
22 Dusty, fusty or musty
23 British P.M. before and after Addington
24 Blah
25 Lower
26 Statements for the record
29 Aim
30 Steps in a ballroom
33 Puts the kibosh on
36 Underground rock bands?
38 Where Etihad Airways is headquartered
41 ___ Tunes
44 One of the knights of the Round Table
49 Acid/alcohol compound
50 Excited pupil's shout
51 Art genre for Man Ray
52 Punjabi chief
54 Weakens
55 W competitor
56 ___ Vogue magazine
58 Go to waste
59 Day ___

by Ian Livengood

14

ACROSS

1 Sister brand of Scope
6 Like blackjack hands with an ace counted as 11
10 Feature of a modern zoo
14 Athlete who uses steroids
15 Decorative enamelware
17 With 34-, 40- and 60-Across, a somber message for our loyal fans
19 Led astray
20 Agrostologists' study
21 Bud
22 "Whoopee!"
23 Letters before Kitty Hawk
26 Feet, in slang
29 Fruit with yellow skin
34 See 17-Across
37 The Gaels of collegiate sports
38 Actress Issa ___ of "The Misadventures of Awkward Black Girl"
39 Shield from the elements
40 See 17-Across
45 Make less flat
46 You might put stock in it
47 Gloaming, to a sonneteer
48 2 letters
50 Pennsylvania and others: Abbr.
52 Inability to sense smells
56 Vigorous reprimand
60 See 17-Across
62 Large marine fish tanks
63 Cardio option
64 "___ Darkness Fall" (L. Sprague de Camp novel)
65 Chew (out)
66 Collects a DNA sample from, say

DOWN

1 Parimutuel calculation
2 Marquis de Sade, e.g.
3 Made like
4 Pause
5 Fancy fabric
6 Long-range guided missile

7 "___ New Hampshire" (state song)
8 Not clear
9 Closet organizer
10 Comfy footwear
11 Responsibility
12 Play money?
13 1980 Oscar nominee directed by Roman Polanski
16 Patronize, as a hotel
18 Later in the text
23 Capital of the Roman province of Africa
24 Coast
25 "Sí" man?
27 Sandwich topped with tzatziki sauce
28 Goes up, up, up

30 ___ bath
31 Blow away
32 Comedian who married Joyce Mathews in 1941, divorced her in 1947 and married her again in 1949 "because she reminded me of my first wife"
33 Winter X Games host city
35 Curiosity org.
36 Overhaul
41 Thing with a filament
42 Online course
43 Holiday a month before Passover
44 Pulls out
49 Military group

51 Drinker's bender?
52 Taking unauthorized R&R
53 "Good going!"
54 Shouts of support
55 Crib part
56 Go here and there
57 Bay or gray follower
58 His .366 lifetime batting average is the best ever
59 Yahtzee category
61 Quinceañera invitee

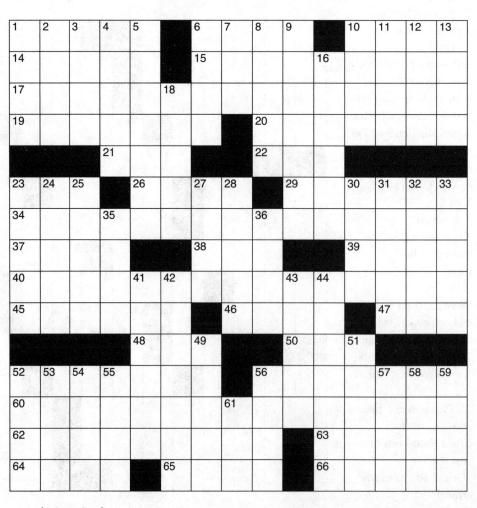

by Peter Gordon

ACROSS

1 Blue period?
7 Pet that needs a sitter?
13 Best Actor Oscar nominee for "The Lion in Winter"
14 Oriental blossom
15 Sartre's first novel
16 What you might get a distorted picture from?
17 Tee off
18 Detective fiction author Paretsky
19 Fragrance created by Fabergé
20 Scoring low on the excite-o-meter
21 Rarely missed stroke
23 Fore-and-aft-rigged vessel
24 Country ___ & Suites
26 Fictional biographer
28 "___ Will Be Loved" (Maroon 5 hit)
29 Restaurant critic who lent his name to a brand at the supermarket
32 Show authority?
34 Lightens up, say
36 Service station offering
39 "Beauty and the Beast" lyricist Howard
40 Macabre
42 Obedience school command
44 Foundry supply
46 Rolled item
47 Tribal title
48 Scorecard figures
49 Unpaid interest?
51 Ontario town across from Buffalo
53 Electrify
54 Club that "even God can't hit," according to Lee Trevino
55 It's not common knowledge
56 Worker at a station
57 Dirty

DOWN

1 "Hasn't scratched yet!" product
2 Concluded
3 Ring for dessert
4 Pharmacological amount
5 Bright-eyed
6 Parliamentary vote
7 Horne of "The Lady and Her Music"
8 "I can finally relax!"
9 Nonhuman explorer
10 Woos
11 "This being the case . . ."
12 Get a mouthful?
14 Side lights?
16 Grammy-nominated rock band for "Epic"
18 Setting of many pirate stories
22 Stirs
23 Gave a leg up to?
25 Fly in the ointment
27 At one's disposal
30 Renaissance Faire garment
31 Reputed
33 One who gets no credit?
35 Salt Lake City daily
36 Demand
37 FaceTime device
38 Raised
41 Security system component
43 Shenanigan
45 Gather together for stitching
48 Kind of plane
50 1977 horror film set in Newfoundland
52 Timeline segment
53 Listing on a Rolodex

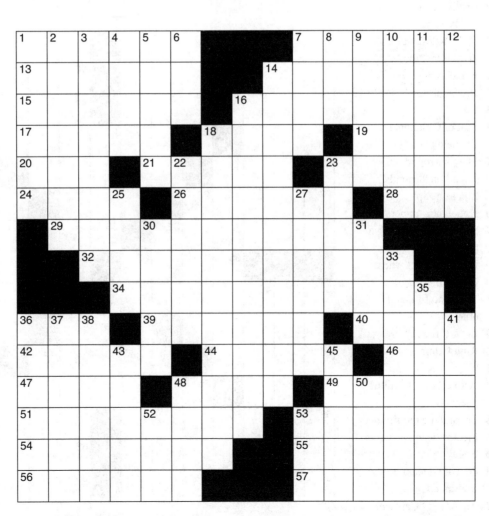

by Patrick Berry

ACROSS

1 Artificial eyelashes, informally
8 Things with round numbers?
15 Reply to a pushy person
16 Far out?
17 Not flirting with your friend's girlfriend, e.g.
18 Gets crushed by, say
19 "Cats" monogram
20 Peaceful protests
22 Athletic great whose name and jersey number rhyme
23 I Samuel preceder
25 Point ___, Calif.
26 Problem on a record
27 Really get to
29 Yankee opposer
30 Color whose name is French for "mole"
31 It may represent November
33 Quit
35 Seat of Oklahoma's Garfield County
37 They surround lenses
38 Friend on "Friends"
42 Zip, as a Ziploc, say
46 Angel hair toppers?
47 Shout while shaking a pompom
49 Friend of Buckwheat
50 Give out
51 The band fun. and others
53 Look through?
54 Ring letters
55 "Take it easy, bro!"
57 "Odi et ___" (Catullus poem)
58 Beyond the requirement
60 Electronic music genre
62 Bogey
63 Pouring poison into a stream, e.g.
64 Answer to "Capisce?"
65 Spicy cuisine

DOWN

1 Plant seen on the Sistine Chapel ceiling
2 In an ordinary fashion
3 Shower clothes
4 Quotation qualifier
5 Teenage dream?
6 "Star Wars" moon
7 In any way
8 Certain pop music fan of the 2010s
9 Cellular transmitters
10 Bygone sportscaster Hodges
11 ___ Styles, lead character in "Boyz N the Hood"
12 Screwdriver selection
13 Gotham building-climbing tool
14 Expressed derision
21 Sized up
24 One low on dough
26 Big wind
28 Keeps a watch on
30 Kept a watch on?
32 Bagel
34 "Right honourable" sort
36 Behind
38 Treat for a dog
39 Treat for a dog
40 Things you can assume
41 Skate park fixture
43 All over the place
44 California's so-called "Island City"
45 Make public
48 Poker variant
51 Low par
52 Angel hair topper
55 Quicken Loans Arena cagers
56 ___ One (2013 release)
59 Pounded paste
61 Zymurgy, e.g.: Abbr.

by David Steinberg

ACROSS

1 Too-clever-by-half type
12 Important school fig.
15 Taunt to a head-turner
16 Head-butter
17 Make an Amazon visit, say
18 Thoughtful gift?
19 Lady, for one
20 What a pacer may be experiencing
22 Project Mercury primate
23 Still red, say
25 Flier not found in 49 states
26 Conform to the party line?
27 Salon job, for short
29 Hallmark occasion
33 Chinese Fireball or Norwegian Ridgeback, in Harry Potter
35 Reproductive couple
36 Sharp shooter?
37 Music style featuring accordions
38 They play by themselves
39 Co-star of TV's "thirtysomething"
40 Trickery
41 A unit
43 Years abroad
44 Moose predator
48 Broad in tastes
50 Like silt vis-à-vis sand
51 Years __
52 "Have some fun!"
55 Fox coverage that may be controversial?
56 What shoulders are often used for
57 Some M.I.T. deg. holders
58 It has many cells

DOWN

1 Hit, old-style
2 Sausalito's county
3 Increase
4 Casting needs
5 Roller on a carriageway
6 __-hoo
7 Many a Weird Al Yankovic title
8 Cause of a rash response?
9 "Got me"
10 Pick up, as ice cubes
11 Crocheter's purchase
12 Title food in children's literature
13 Crashed
14 Tour gear
21 Relative of Sinhalese
23 Event with goat tying
24 Santa __ (weather phenomena)
26 Tony
28 Holiday spots?
29 Doofus
30 Lions, Tigers and Bears play in it
31 Cold remedies?
32 Depression shared by soldiers
33 Hills' counterparts
34 Amazonas and Nilo
36 Certain plea, for short
38 Not faking it
40 Legal release
42 Bad things to find in theories
44 Singer's concern
45 Let loose
46 Row with many people
47 "Give it __!"
48 Monk's on "Seinfeld," e.g.
49 Definitely not step lively
50 Bass parts
53 Turkish chief
54 Set the pace

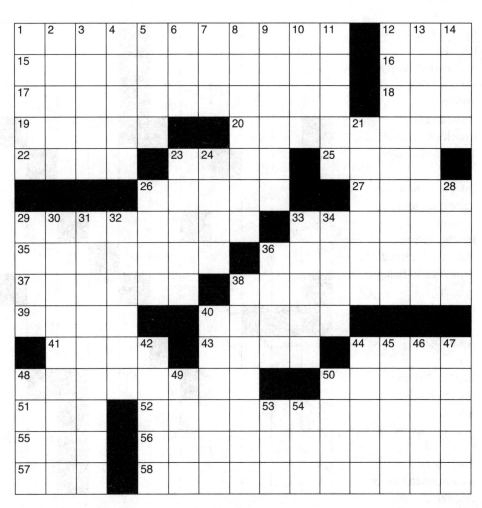

by Robyn Weintraub

18

ACROSS

1 Graveyard hour
7 Dark as dark can be
15 Nova Scotia, once
16 Not excessively
17 A ghostwriter isn't given one
18 Ball
19 Haggis ingredient
20 "What's hangin'?"
21 It comes to a head
22 Ursule, e.g.: Abbr.
23 Means of tracking wildlife
26 Old radio dummy
27 Squeaker in a cage
30 City on the Oka River
31 Arles article
32 Lucky strike
35 Result of holding or hooking
37 Shot-putter's activity
39 Latin word on a diploma
40 Dedicated to
41 Conclusion lead-in
42 Tropical smoothie flavor
45 Double-dipping, e.g.
48 Answering to
49 ___ Balls
50 Healing helper
51 Show that's earned more than 40 Emmys, in brief
52 Lack of anxiety
54 Spreadsheet function
56 Sonnet-ending unit
58 72 of its 108 lines end in "-ore" sounds
59 "The Evangelist" of Christianity
60 Book that doesn't require much time or thought
61 "But still . . ."

DOWN

1 Dynamite
2 Hostile looks
3 A 99¢ burger may be on it
4 "Desperate Housewives" housewife
5 Slangy "True, no?"
6 Questel who voiced Olive Oyl
7 Fitting gifts for puzzle enthusiasts?
8 "Uncle!"
9 Too much, to Marcel
10 See 38-Down
11 Valentino type
12 Fourth-wall breaker
13 Star on the horizon?
14 Work digitally?
22 Fill time at an airport, say
24 Symbols of change, in math
25 Shot from behind the arc, informally
26 Shot putter's supply?
28 Grist for a war of words?
29 Ageless, ages ago
33 It often catches an infection
34 Rail heads
36 "OMG, I'm cracking up!"
37 Place for a stove light
38 With 10-Down, turn in
40 First country in the world with universal suffrage (1906)
43 Product of natural outdoor steeping
44 Onetime motel come-on
45 Refinement
46 Warm welcome?
47 Snoozers
51 Relief pitcher's success
53 Pistolet ou canon
55 "God, home and country" org.
56 Literary monogram
57 Fight call, for short

by Andrew Kingsley

ACROSS

1 Holder of many titles
12 Show with the record for most Emmys won in a single year (12)
14 Encountered trouble
16 Snags
17 What a star may represent
18 Non-Rx
19 Rx abbr.
20 Locales for deep investigations?
25 "We should get going"
29 Home to the naturally pink Lake Retba
30 Attended as an observer
31 It's spanned by the Ponte Santa Trinita
32 Army ___
33 Allison Janney's role on "The West Wing"
36 Architect/sculpt or with an eponymous New York museum
40 Control and make use of
41 Big name in late-night
42 Topkapi Palace resident
43 Choler
44 Deadline in a western
49 Anticipate
53 Turn lemons into lemonade, so to speak
55 Countercharge
56 Help someone

DOWN

1 M.R.I. alternative
2 "The Zone of Interest" author, 2014
3 Seat of Washoe County
4 Spoil, with "on"
5 Some successful Wharton grads, for short
6 Sports person: Abbr.
7 G
8 They may be graphic
9 Some temperatures
10 Go ___ length
11 Bronze
12 Relative of a soul patch
13 Commences
14 Luster
15 Transcribe
21 Get into one's head
22 Tally
23 Mamie Eisenhower hairstyle
24 Grinds
25 Info in a 1-Across
26 Means of divination
27 Put on
28 Showed great happiness
33 It might be yawning
34 Luxury car name since 1935
35 Started, as a generator
37 Lingerie material
38 Speedball component
39 Like atoms with full outer shells
45 Miami Beach architectural style, informally
46 ___ vez (again: Sp.)
47 Clay, for one
48 Friend of Bubbles, in an animated film
49 Hang
50 Focus of some prep books
51 Battle of ___ (1943 U.S./ Japanese conflict)
52 Rouge alternative
54 Thumbnail item

by Julian Lim

ACROSS

1 Bedroom set piece?
14 Band with the 2012 double-platinum album "Night Visions"
16 Celebrity with the fashion line "V."
18 Internet issue
19 Hacking it
20 One tailed in the sewers
21 Want
22 Flares
24 "___ on my bed my limbs I lay" (line from Coleridge)
25 Fill with horror
27 It has a good resolution
28 Lose energy
31 "Di quella pira," e.g.
32 Tigerlike
34 "___ life belongs to those who live in the present": Wittgenstein
36 Chinese province where a spicy cuisine originated
37 Swear
38 Fitness center?
39 Half of a couple
40 Doesn't shut up
41 Targets of President Taft
43 Big maker of 27-Acrosses
44 Souvenir item
46 Unlikely swinger
50 Org. with a name registration
51 Captain ___ (DC Comics superhero)
52 Lacking subtlety, say
53 Extra sauce order?
57 Match.com competitors
58 Jibber-jabbers

DOWN

1 Jeremy of "Entourage"
2 Leave speechless
3 Girl with a gun in an Aerosmith hit
4 What a chair covers
5 ___ en scène
6 Puzzle hunt?: Abbr.
7 "___ dear . . ."
8 Big name in energy bars and smoothies
9 Like some councils
10 It may be running
11 Checks out
12 "J'accuse!" reply
13 Punch line instrument
15 Little something for the road?
17 Piano-playing Cat
22 Sardine relative
23 Beach mold
26 Slams
27 Snarky syllable
28 Distillery eponym Joseph
29 Mud spot?
30 Wreak vengeance on
32 "That's a ___!"
33 Celebrity whose name sounds like a drink
35 Thing, at bar
36 Bad way to turn
38 ___ Peninsula (2014 crisis site)
41 Some beachwear
42 Neat
44 Source of the words "curry" and "pariah"
45 Perform poorly
47 Apply, as Bengay
48 Lies around
49 Chuckleheads
52 Takes in
54 H
55 Opposite of hence
56 Place of corruption

by David Phillips and David Steinberg

ACROSS

1 "I hear you"
10 Flub
15 Smell-O-Vision competitor of 1950s cinema
16 Sound of an everyday explosion
17 Order-flouting protester
18 Butler who was expelled from West Point
19 It welcomes compliments
20 Evil Queen's disguise in "Snow White and the Seven Dwarfs"
21 Pops up
23 Decked out
25 Accouterment for a diva
26 Isle named for a Gaelic goddess
27 Opposing group
28 Best Actress winner for "Klute"
30 Narrow waterway
31 Male offspring, in Munich
32 1992 Olympic figure skating silver medalist
33 Good place to vent
35 Restaurant breakfast innovation of 1971
38 Alternatives to Bartletts
40 Mate 4 life?
41 Many a charity run
44 Paltry amount
45 Squinting cartoon character
47 Add with a beater
48 Curly-tailed dogs
50 Office page?
51 World's second-largest retailer
52 Hit the roof
54 Esquire's target audience
55 Advent time: Abbr.
56 Tiny hairs
57 Item in the lobby of a country inn
60 Peterhof Palace personages
61 11-Down, e.g.

62 Kids' classic that opens "His mother was ugly and his father was ugly"
63 Prized

DOWN

1 Noble at the end of a table?
2 Sauce seasoning
3 Attack viciously
4 Prey for a dingo
5 Roseola symptoms
6 Where the rubber meets the road
7 Chill (with)
8 Renoir vis-à-vis Monet
9 Go up against
10 Lead-in to bones or knuckles
11 Canyon colour
12 Approachable, unglamorous sort
13 Algonquin Round Table, e.g.
14 Pressure cooker
22 Big name in financial fraud
24 "Correct!"
25 Music player for a break dancer
28 Org. with scam alerts
29 "Ariadne __ Naxos"
32 Comforting words to a worried loved one
34 South American monkeys
36 Impulse buy at a checkout counter
37 "The Day the Earth Stood Still" craft
38 Parts
39 Foster
42 "Impressive!"
43 Bad-mouthed
46 Many an infomercial offering
47 Three in a quarter
49 Burj Khalifa feature
51 Jai alai basket
53 Mission
54 Piddling
58 Former Mideast org.
59 Grill measure, in brief

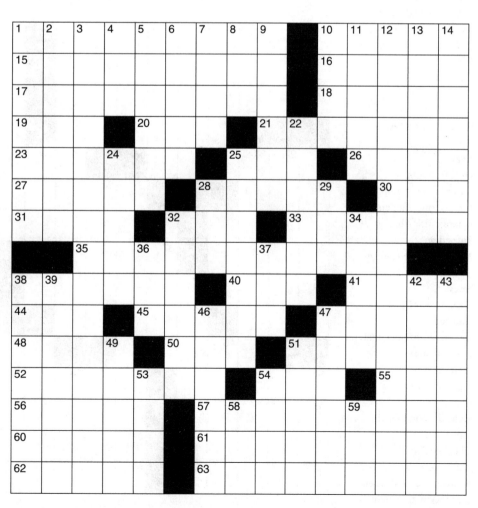

by Kristian House

22

ACROSS

1 Anagrams
10 Spoke hesitantly
15 "Who the hell does he think he is?!"
16 Like basil leaves
17 Italian for "sleeves"
18 Phylum, order or genus
19 Don ___, 1956 World Series M.V.P.
20 Comportments
21 "Bluebeard's Castle" composer
24 Drives
26 Letters in some church names
27 Half-cup measures
29 Kind of classic rock?
32 Coin of Iran
34 Attraction temporarily shut down and partly moved to Siberia during W.W. II
36 Eye
37 Longtime "All My Children" role
38 Mazar of "Entourage"
39 Rule in a kids' outdoor game
41 Lead
42 Old atlas inits.
43 Cameos, for example
44 Like Bernie Sanders, before 2015: Abbr.
45 Turned up
47 Mountain bike features
50 Swell
52 Swell
55 Capital near Lake Titicaca
56 First novel of the Great Plains trilogy
60 "Smart" guy
61 Lead singer for the Cars
62 Hybrid woman-bird monster
63 The "thee" in Shakespeare's line "But I do love thee! and when I love thee not, / Chaos is come again"

DOWN

1 Personal ad designation
2 Chinese tea
3 Published
4 Not straight up
5 Gambling mecca
6 Single-named musical artist
7 Do-overs
8 Single-named artist
9 They're marked with X's
10 Total wreck
11 Benefit
12 Uses flowery language
13 Kind of blue that's close to green
14 Animal shelters
21 Magna Carta drafters
22 Title trio in a 1986 comedy
23 One unlikely to punk out
25 Aids in raising arms?
27 Onetime political leader with a museum in Grand Rapids, Mich.
28 How beer at a cookout might be kept
30 Protect from an overflow, in a way
31 Alternatives to 'Vettes
33 Bucolic setting
34 Simon of Duran Duran
35 Goals of some drives, for short
40 Nine-time Hart Memorial Trophy winner
46 Image Awards grp.
47 Wasn't overturned
48 Starting now
49 Early hour
50 Not so hot
51 When repeated, part of Van Morrison's "Brown Eyed Girl"
53 Cap-___ (from head to toe)
54 Motor problems
57 That: Sp.
58 Kylo ___ of "Star Wars"
59 Mighty Mighty Bosstones genre

by Damon Gulczynski

ACROSS

1 Singer with the 1977 hit "Lido Shuffle"
7 Things with roots
13 House of Tybalt and Juliet
15 "Under the Lilacs" writer, 1878
16 Eastern border of Manhattan's Tompkins Square Park
17 Staple of Caribbean music
18 Car mentioned in "Hotel California," informally
20 Eponymous bacteriologist Julius
21 Nickname for Francisco
22 The so-called "sunny side"
24 Cold-shoulder
25 Many a circus feat
27 7-Eleven, e.g.
29 Steven Van Zandt's role on "The Sopranos," informally
30 Constantly adjusting one's glasses, e.g.
32 Back on track?
34 Who said "There is nothing more deceptive than an obvious fact"
38 Wing man?
39 1977 reggae classic
40 So-so
41 Concert stage effect
42 Polemologists study them
44 Wiriness
48 Same-sex household?
50 "I deny all that!"
52 Artist Thomas ___, founder of the Hudson River School
53 Bowls are seen in them
55 Harebrained
57 Creative classroom
59 Put one's foot down, in a way
60 "Right-o"
61 Rock candy, essentially
62 Give one's blessing
63 Lounging spot

DOWN

1 Little rascals
2 But
3 Illuminating comment
4 Something a politician proposes that takes heat?
5 Archivist's supply
6 Slummy
7 Who sings "As Time Goes By" in "Casablanca"
8 Thunderous noise
9 End of many a farm name
10 Execrable
11 2000s retro Chrysler
12 Kind of steel
14 Building bar with one flange
19 Sign at a concession stand
23 Katharine ___, onetime publisher of the Washington Post
26 So far, informally
28 Hits on the side . . . or cuts from the back
31 Agemate
33 Andrew Jackson nickname
34 Jaywalkers, e.g.
35 Payments to speakers, say
36 With beauty and class
37 Common character in Dungeons & Dragons
43 Low class
45 Casual response to "Thanks"
46 Title six-year-old of literature
47 Made damp
49 Where to watch the Beeb
51 Cousin of "Skoal!"
54 "The 120 Days of Sodom" author
56 Colombian crop
58 Team on which Larry Bird played, on scoreboards

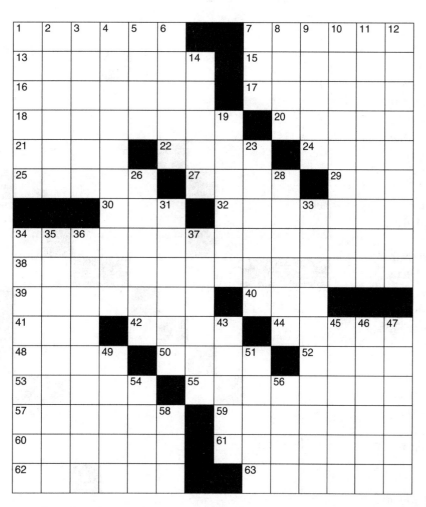

by Josh Knapp

ACROSS

1 Popular website with virtual animals
8 Met for a party?
16 Film villain who says "Your feeble skills are no match for the power of the dark side"
18 Classic conflict
19 Confederate
20 Bold way to solve a crossword
21 Some AOL exchanges
22 Like teddies, often
23 Source of some leather
25 Wheel that runs?
26 Rat-___
27 Feckless
28 Beau
29 Tough to get ahold of
30 Boots one
31 Anytown, U.S.A., sign
32 Something hot
34 "___ on Fire" (2012 Alicia Keys hit)
35 Executor's charge
38 Camp invader
40 Bellwether's "belles"
44 Carried
45 Put on hold
46 Get-out-of-jail aid, maybe
47 Go without saying?
48 Route through the boondocks
49 Protein-rich paste
50 ___ Tamid (synagogue lamp)
51 Raiser of horses?
52 Like some cakes
53 Classic R&B hit about a returning lover
57 It has multiple clauses
58 Honey
59 Post-Impressionist Seurat

DOWN

1 Very distant clouds
2 Issue
3 Like spectroscopes and microscopes
4 Dictatorial boss
5 Director ___ C. Kenton
6 Prominent feature of a sloth
7 Sign adored by angels
8 Brief refreshers
9 "The Green Hornet" trumpeter
10 Stand on its head
11 Holder of spirits
12 Literally, "land of the sun"
13 Second club used on a par 4 hole, maybe
14 Adams and Jefferson, e.g.
15 Final order of things?
17 Big name in drugs
23 Feudal lord
24 Memo starter
25 Beer-and-whiskey cocktail
28 ". . . let slip the dogs of ___": Shak.
31 Stuck
33 Grabbed something
34 Black-tie event
35 Vernacular much debated in the 1990s
36 By hook or by crook
37 Ancient Greek craft
38 Island north of Antigua
39 Tablet contents, perhaps
41 Not yet admitted
42 Heart
43 They hold water
45 Power in old films
48 Purchase in large quantity
51 Medium gait
52 Twice quattuor
54 Wild way to go
55 Bit of blood-typing shorthand
56 21st word of the Pledge of Allegiance

by David Steinberg

25

ACROSS

1 Longtime "Mike & Mike" airer
10 See 29-Across
15 Utterly
16 Not act conservatively
17 Sets in
18 Widespread unrest
19 Got on a roll?
20 Plot element
21 "Gimme a break" product
22 First name in 39-Down research
24 God with green skin
26 Where "crossword" is "korsord": Abbr.
27 Good-sized combo
29 With 10-Across, player that the Broncos replaced with Peyton Manning
30 Like ___ of corn (really easy)
31 Something given to Apple's Siri
35 Like much locker room language
37 Things to cry over?
38 Samsung Galaxy rival
40 Tabula ___
41 Audio receiver
42 Mountain climbers?
46 Exemplar of ease
47 Hub for All Nippon Airways
50 Sports great with the 1993 memoir "Days of Grace"
51 Place for billiards or bingo
53 Forum rule enforcers, for short
55 Neptune vis-à-vis Saturn
56 Fajita option
57 Halves of twinsets
59 Early growth areas
60 Assurance that you can get bread at a store
61 One with eye patches
62 Well-rooted course?

DOWN

1 Tabasco, por ejemplo
2 Reception annoyance
3 Nudge
4 Hanoi-to-Beijing dir.
5 Chill out
6 Potential reaction to a cat
7 Makes a dead duck
8 "Sure, tell me"
9 Matchless?
10 Actress Polo and others
11 Shoot out
12 Project Gutenberg job
13 Senators' supporters, largely
14 Home to the Royal Opera House
21 Wear for Japan's Coming of Age Day
23 State with the most mountain ranges
25 Big name in projectors
28 Big name in mowers
30 One multiplying by division
32 "Really!"
33 French film award
34 Pristine
35 Panini bread
36 Not in real life, say
38 Finishes
39 Person, e.g.
43 Go after
44 Girl in a Beach Boys hit
45 Saw, say
47 Lumia smartphone launcher
48 The "Velvet" half of jazz's "Velvet & Brass"
49 "___ to the list"
52 Fatten
54 Things laid on scapegoats
57 Hotel waiter?
58 Fed. purchasing agency

by Zhouqin Burnikel

26

ACROSS

1 Fan group?
7 Centerpiece of a holiday gathering
14 The "R" of E.R.
15 No-parking area in a parking lot
16 Holiday cupful
17 Brought out of hibernation
18 Stock
19 Boxing ring producer
20 Worker with a saving plan, for short
21 Dog team's burden
22 With 40-Across, exposed
23 Cricket field shape
24 The American Messenger Co., today
25 Racketeering outfit
26 Drip chamber contents
28 Idled
31 "I'm counting on you!"
33 Harold Hill's portrayer in the original cast of "The Music Man"
35 Bugs
37 Lemon oil source
38 Green on a screen
39 Most important part
40 See 22-Across
41 Wild catch?
42 Rested
43 Party spread
44 Garden assets
45 Test of effectiveness
48 Bright yellow fruit
49 Some Kings' Scholars
50 Exceeding the usual rate
51 Like the papacy of Pius IX, after St. Peter
52 Another name for Michaelmas daisies

DOWN

1 Creates, as trouble
2 Yellow pages?
3 Hostile territory?
4 Took courses
5 Genesis grandson
6 Succumb to gravity
7 Admit defeat
8 Eurasian boundary
9 Dr. Kildare portrayer Ayres
10 Longtime band with the 2015 album "Alone in the Universe"
11 Los Angeles suburb next to San Fernando
12 Very small, as an operation
13 Gradual, as a slope
15 They're good for the long haul
19 Talk show talk
22 Cafeteria utensils
23 "American Me" star, 1992
25 Do well enough
26 Tristram Shandy's creator
27 Came through for
29 High-hat
30 TV drama starring Terrence Howard
32 It begins with All Saints' Day
34 Offers objections to
35 Brewery named for a Dutch river
36 Approaching
40 Principal force
41 Presuppose
43 Two-piece tops
44 Private engagements?
46 First name of 2012's Best Director
47 Misrepresentation
48 1040 preparer, for short

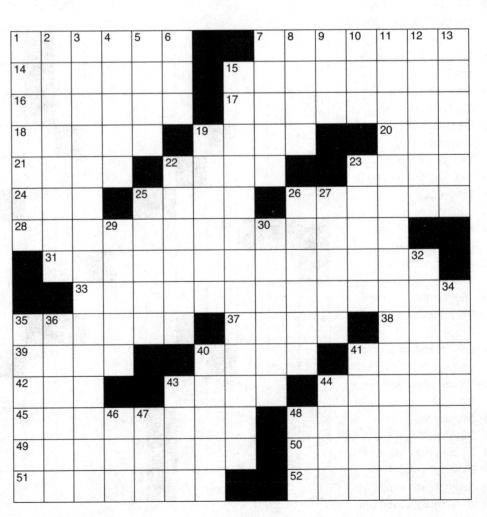

by Patrick Berry

ACROSS

1 Talk
7 Driver's hazards
15 Not divisible, as a job
16 Amelia Earhart, e.g.
17 Good news for wage earners
18 Far Eastern city whose name means "long cape"
19 Org. that covers Springfield in a dome in "The Simpsons Movie"
20 Torpedo
22 Black
23 Office monitor
25 Dough made in the Middle East?
26 Lane in a strip
27 Wedding keepsake
29 Long-running Vegas show
30 Even's opposite
31 Gravy goody
33 Mississippi feeder
35 Backslash neighbor
39 Buddhist memorial dome
40 Like motets
42 Cross words
44 One-on-one basketball play, slangily
46 Sound
47 Feature of un poema
48 Accomplished
50 Damage done
51 It welcomes praise
52 "Wouldn't think so"
54 Pixar specialty, briefly
55 City called the Bush Capital
57 2006 musical featuring a vampire
59 Light blue partner of Connecticut and Vermont
60 Crazy Horse, e.g.
61 "It was my pleasure"
62 They're drawn by the bizarre

DOWN

1 Green grocery choice
2 Brazilian city name that sounds like a U.S. state capital
3 Some southern cookin'
4 Alternative to SHO
5 Celebrate
6 Rapping response
7 Its rosters aren't real
8 1997 comedy with the tagline "Trust me"
9 Odysseus' faithful dog
10 Clout
11 Christmas trio
12 Key of Chopin's étude "Tristesse"
13 Collect lots of
14 Cross states
21 Word with a 35-Across before and after it
24 Separator of the Philippines and Malaysia
26 "Incoming!"
28 Charcuterie, e.g.
30 Nut-brown
32 Tony-winning title role of 1990
34 Country's __ Brown Band
36 Aid in labor management?
37 One handling an OD
38 Get too close, in a way
41 Teases, in older usage
42 French daily, with "Le"
43 Lackey's response
45 Pick
47 Casing job, for short
48 Big supply line
49 Bill collectors?
52 Dimple
53 Something farm-squeezed?
56 Arthur with a Tony
58 Genre for Reel Big Fish

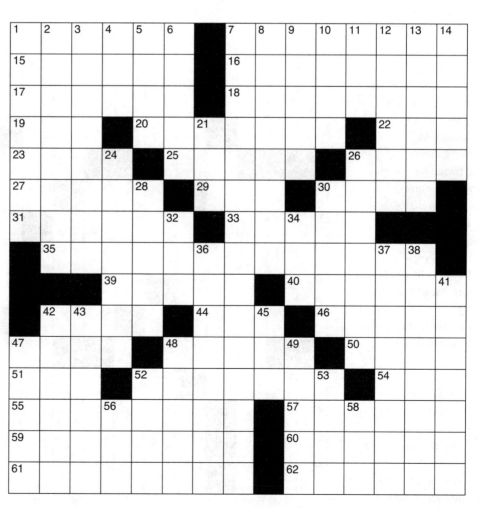

by James Mulhern

ACROSS

1 Preceder of 64-Across on the calendar
12 It may justify things
15 Ilmenite is the chief one
16 Winner of the first three Fiesta Bowls, for short
17 Airport terminal feature
18 Radio frequency abbr.
19 Scrap
20 Discoverer of New Zealand
21 "I can't believe that!"
22 Liberty's home, for short
23 4-Downs, south of the border
25 Site of Akbar the Great's tomb
28 Article in El País
31 Release?
34 Parts of cross-shaped churches
37 He worked for Hershey in the 1910s–'20s
38 Quaint getaway destination
40 Bring down
41 Officially gives up
42 More compact
44 Dutch oven, e.g.
45 1995 Emmy winner Sofer
46 Less adorned
48 Highway hazard
50 Laverne and Shirley, e.g.
52 Lumber mill employee
55 World of Warcraft figure
58 Bud abroad
59 Port authority?
61 World of Warcraft figure
62 Name that went down in history?
63 Buns, for example
64 Follower of 1-Across on the calendar

DOWN

1 Vitamin a.k.a. riboflavin
2 Story teller
3 Having a scrap
4 Stealthy sort
5 Sweaters and such
6 Got via guile
7 Kirmans, e.g.
8 Certain prayer leader
9 Rapper wrapper?
10 22-Across and others
11 Motion supporter
12 Departs
13 Court legend
14 Dreaded game show sound
21 Antedate
22 Civil War battle site
24 Largest minority in Bulgaria
25 Single chance?
26 Duck lookalike
27 Spots for air traffic controllers
29 They may precede high-speed chases, in brief
30 Peel
32 European city whose name means "eat"
33 Bright swimmer
35 Part of a mean mien
36 One of Utah's state symbols
39 Civil War battle site
43 Like hashish or shoe wax
47 Soul mate?
49 Philosophy
50 Bookkeeper's stamp
51 It's loaded
53 "___ live!"
54 W.W. I battle site
55 With 60-Down, gotten by great effort
56 "Eri tu," but not "Eres Tú"
57 Oz salutation
59 New Mexico State's athletic grp.
60 See 55-Down

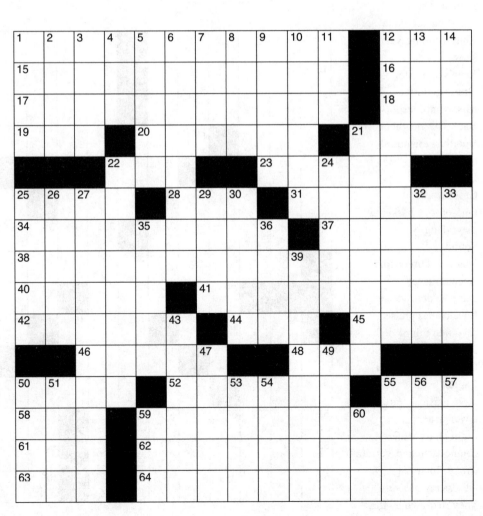

by Barry C. Silk

ACROSS

1 Insincerely polite
7 13-Down natives, e.g.
15 Hugh who played TV's House
16 Laid into
17 Wool source
18 Subcontinent-wide
19 One for whom 36-Across has four syllables
21 Many new car drivers
22 Island west of Mull
23 Red stuff to cut through
25 Dim bulbs
26 Off
28 Compromise
30 Trial cover-up
31 Gray head
32 Has the stage
34 What exterior doors typically do
36 See 19- and 57-Across
38 Lyricist who adapted "Pygmalion"
41 Clubs to beat people with?
42 Chrome runners, maybe
45 x, y and z
46 Mozart title starter
48 Devil's deck
50 Lawyer's workload
52 Admission evidence
54 Musical group known for wearing red hats called "energy domes"
55 Recycling bin fill
57 One for whom 36-Across has three syllables
59 Figure-changing agent
61 Calmer?
62 Lesser "Seinfeld" role played by Len Lesser
63 Bomb
64 Early Beatle
65 Going rates

DOWN

1 Beyond slow
2 Sought safety, say
3 Princess in line to the British throne after Beatrice
4 Agents in some therapy
5 When told "I'm sleepy," she sometimes says "I hope you're not driving"
6 Rising generation?
7 The Era of ___ (1964–74 Notre Dame football)
8 Like some angels and arches
9 Really bug
10 Paris fights in it
11 Like many bad words
12 Appended
13 Safari Capital of the World
14 Nine-time presidential contender of the 1940s–'90s
20 Shaving the beard with a razor, in Jewish law
24 Bit of décor in a sports bar
27 It makes a wave
29 Nap
33 Top of the line?
35 Tick, e.g.
36 Fill with anxiety
37 Freeze
38 Like skates and corsets
39 Scrutinize
40 Word repeatedly spelled out by Franklin
42 Make as a heat-and-serve product, say
43 Much-sought-after
44 British floors
47 Time after Time?
49 Think much of
51 Backtrack?
53 Calligraphic messes
56 Creator of the lawyer Perry
58 "Superman" catchphrase starter
60 Grokked

by Matt Ginsberg

30

ACROSS

1 Sharp projections
5 What a capt. may aspire to be
8 Service provider
14 Much-photographed mausoleum site
15 1978 Grammy nominee Chris
16 Be faithful (to)
17 Blotchy, in a way
18 Blotchy, in a way
20 Mimicking
21 "Enfantines" composer
22 "Join the club"
23 Lifesaver, at times
24 Book and film title character surnamed Gatzoyiannis
25 Flame proof?
26 Fancy wrap
28 Measure of econ. health
30 Gear protector
33 Got rich
39 Depression era?
40 One with a smaller Indian relative
41 Hurtful pair in a playground rhyme
42 Show celerity
43 Flop's opposite
44 Mil. roadside hazard
45 78 letters
48 Dixieland sound
51 "10-4"
54 Cole Porter topic
56 "To Helen" writer, in footnotes
57 Feedable thing
58 Abstract Expressionist who married Jackson Pollock
60 Cannery row?
61 Iris feature
62 He's unrefined
63 They're unrefined
64 Brokerage come-on

65 Suffix with green
66 Big name in Renaissance patronage

DOWN

1 Follower of a diet system
2 Twinkle-toed
3 Only living thing that can be seen from outer space
4 Blue
5 Alternative to Geneva
6 Al __
7 Appearing with fanfare
8 Back stroke?
9 "Battlestar Galactica" role
10 Starts suddenly

11 What "Banzai!" literally means
12 Food brand since 1912
13 Fresh styling
19 Who called a date "a job interview that lasts all night"
21 Green around the gills, maybe
27 Shakespearean duel overseer
29 They're often struck in studios
31 Combined
32 Temporary quitting times?
33 Make __ of (botch)
34 Civvies

35 What Google Wallet uses
36 Eternal water-pourers in Hades
37 Chameleon, e.g.
38 Literally, "big water"
46 What some caddies hold
47 __ Norman (cosmetics franchise)
49 21-Across's "Three Pieces in the Shape of __"
50 Circumlocutory
52 Target of the plume trade
53 Western union?
54 War room development
55 Wind-cheating
59 Some camera cells
60 __ College

by Martin Ashwood-Smith and George Barany

ACROSS

1 Gets steamy, with "up"
5 Order to go away
9 Ever
14 Letters on a crucifix
15 Rabbit's friend
16 Grit
17 Teen's fender bender, maybe
20 2001 fantasy/adventure film with three sequels
21 Many an étagère display
22 Gush
23 Lab housing the world's largest machine
24 Luca who "sleeps with the fishes"
25 Symbol of virility
30 Don't delay
31 However
33 "Frozen" princess
34 Match makeup
36 Match
37 "Ellen's Design Challenge" airer
38 One of the eight points of contact in Muay Thai
39 Least apt to offend
41 "Life of Pi" director
42 Longest word in English containing only one vowel
44 Many gases lack them
46 R&B/pop singer Aubrey
47 Readies for an operation
48 Therapist's image
52 Some miniature hors d'oeuvres
54 Concern in family planning
56 Inuit for "house"
57 Simon of the stage
58 Hostile to
59 Roughhouse?
60 Eponyms of the week?
61 270°

DOWN

1 Goes on perfectly
2 Target of the Occupy movement
3 Brains
4 Twisted sorts
5 Figure in a dark suit
6 They're held at both ends when eating
7 Sister co. of Verizon Wireless
8 "How Deep Is Your Love" Grammy winners
9 Principal, e.g.
10 Catacomb component
11 Turn and a half on the ice
12 Shoppers' headache
13 "I'm in!"
18 Cry after "One, two, three," maybe
19 Rail hubs?
23 Intolerantly pious
24 Takes pleasure (in)
25 Deep in thought
26 "Yeah, right!"
27 Like the Bahamas, Barbados and Belize
28 Cuts through
29 "Two thumbs way up!" and such
32 Like losers' looks
35 Get
40 Doughnutlike
43 Kind of pass in basketball
45 Make furniture-safe, in a way
47 Relatives of sprains
48 Relative of a spoonbill
49 Just about
50 African tree cultivated for its nuts
51 Like-minded voters
52 Muslim judge of North Africa
53 Bit of improv
55 Driver of a bus.

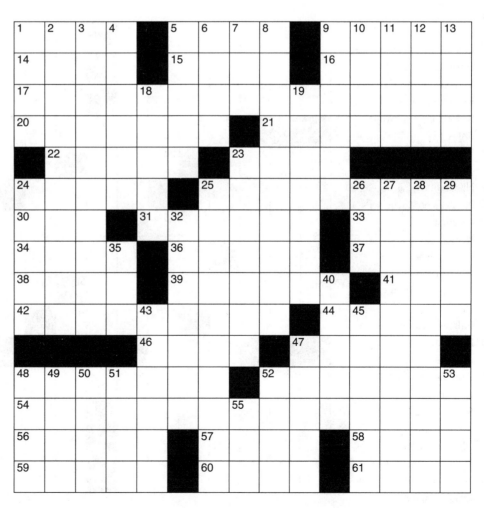

by John Guzzetta

32

ACROSS

1 Conflicts with combat
8 TED talk, e.g.
15 Going around the world?
16 Where people live well beyond the city limits
17 Eponym of an annual Golden Globe award for lifetime achievement
18 Parts of abdomens
19 Event where kids ask lots of questions, informally
21 Hardly deliberate
24 Female antelope
25 Student monitors, for short
26 Like the tops of many porticoes
28 Crib piece
30 Home of Charlie Chan
34 Mortal
36 Recited prayers
38 Second City subway org.
39 You might be thrown on it
41 Narrow inlet
42 Average producer
44 Paradise
46 Recital numbers
47 Sammy who wrote the lyrics to "Ain't That a Kick in the Head"
49 Italian dictators
50 Frustrated cry
52 Impressed cry
54 Dunham of "Girls"
55 Real hack?
60 Resembling a heavy curtain, say
61 Christie's event
65 Temple of Artemis city
66 "Ah, got it"
67 Least hopping
68 Chameleon, e.g.

DOWN

1 Put away
2 "Army of ___" (recruiting slogan)
3 "Spotlight" director McCarthy
4 Twists
5 ___-bodied
6 Sore
7 Some women on "Mad Men"
8 Injured: Fr.
9 Added cost of selling overseas
10 Confessional word
11 Charge that may be high
12 "Evolving the way the world moves" sloganeer
13 Compost heap bit
14 Undemanding
20 Colorful swallow?
21 Some mixtapes
22 Playground comeback
23 Opposite of fine print?
27 Locale for a 39-Across
29 Direct
31 Shooting star?
32 U.S. athlete who won more gold medals at the 1980 Winter Olympics than all but two non-U.S. countries
33 Patriotic chant
35 Martial arts weapons that are two sticks connected by a chain
37 Somewhat
40 Div. of the Justice Department
43 Moved like a 20-Down
45 There's nothing to it
48 "I was robbed!"
51 Come about
53 Mount
55 Armisen of "Portlandia"
56 Hip-hop's ___ Fiasco
57 Ottoman honorific
58 Start and end of many a flight
59 The Miners of the N.C.A.A.
62 What makes nose noise?
63 :-D alternative
64 Source of fleece

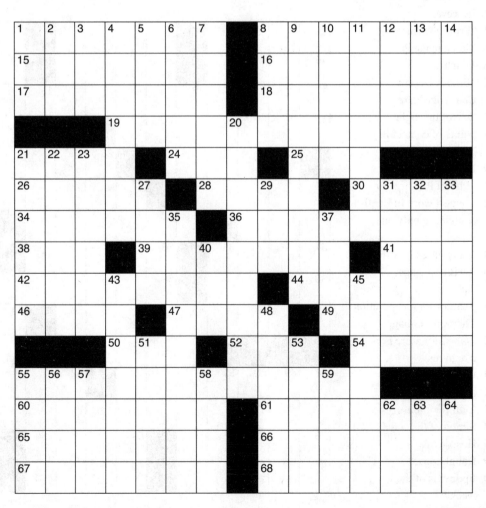

by Brendan Emmett Quigley

ACROSS

1 Porcine paramour
11 Yesterday, so to speak
15 Product with a Crispy Buffalo variety
16 Underwater breather
17 Tremendous
18 Beginning to morph?
19 Brady bunch, briefly
20 Some zoo employees
21 Harmonious
22 Blubbers
23 Some red giants
24 Little 'un
27 They had rolls to play, once
29 Disappearing exclamations
30 Foe of Big Boy and Little Face
33 Tremendously
34 Bothers
35 Bothers
36 Good news for business
38 Combined
39 Turn on
40 Shot measure
41 Meshes
43 One for whom "hello" is "hej"
44 Geezers
45 Tough spots
46 What "it" is found in
49 Symbol del cristianismo
50 Haughty
53 Artist Magritte
54 It takes turns making dinner
55 Extra, in ads
56 Reminder that sticks?

DOWN

1 Sound from a cheater
2 Israel's Olmert
3 Staple of Memorial Day services
4 Instrument that's cradled, for short
5 Full of butterflies
6 Under water
7 Touches
8 Mushy foods
9 '50s campaign nickname
10 2014 World Cup winner: Abbr.
11 Weapon used in the Vietnam War
12 Seriously under the weather
13 Fix as 20-Across might do
14 Schemes
21 "And who ___?"
22 Hot, salty snack
23 Lord & Taylor rival, informally
24 Go over
25 John Paul II, e.g.
26 Do some ferreting
27 Magical duster
28 Founder of Rhyme $yndicate Records
30 Webster wrote many of them: Abbr.
31 Traffic director
32 Nieuwpoort's river
34 Counterpart of moi
37 Some antlered animals
38 "No, no, really . . ."
40 He succeeded two queens
41 Capital up the coast from Cape Coast
42 Hurt with a horn
43 Hoist on a ship
45 Dashes off
46 Pacific dietary staple
47 Settled
48 Jubilation
50 "Leaves and Navels" artist
51 Comic's nightmare?
52 Eli Manning, on the field

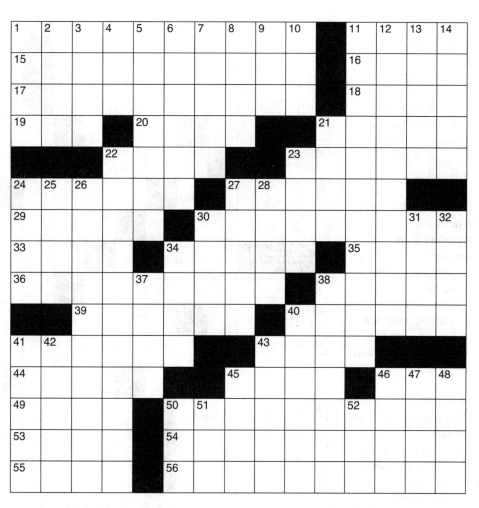

by Kelly Clark

34

ACROSS

1 "Come again?"
10 They're put in for work
15 Brand whose first commercial featured a cable car
16 Large-scale detail
17 Trust issue?
18 "Bleeding Love" singer Lewis
19 Non-humanities acronym
20 When repeated, spouse's complaint
21 Walter ___, Dodgers manager before Tommy Lasorda
22 "The Fox and the Hound" fox
23 Dish that often has pea pods
25 Medium for many 13-Down
26 Emmy-winning Susan Lucci role
28 "On the hoof," in diner lingo
29 "Yeah, why not!?"
30 Kim Jong-un, for one
32 Gendered "Seinfeld" accessory
34 Shake off
36 Sticky stuff
37 Person with a lot on his plate?
41 [I find this mildly amusing]
45 Confederate
46 Rush, e.g.
48 Corners
49 Federal div. concerned with gas consumption
50 They may be settled over drinks
52 Burn
53 Shakes off
55 "If you ask me . . . ," for short
56 Give a Yelp review, say
57 Hometown of Columbus
58 "Let's do this!"
60 Secluded spaces
61 "Let's do this!"

62 Yom Kippur War leader
63 America, informally

DOWN

1 Took by force
2 Done for
3 Was on the cast of
4 ___ U.S.A.
5 Sr. stress source
6 Reznor of Nine Inch Nails
7 What blowhards blow
8 On end, to Donne
9 Concert needs, for short
10 Good for sledding, say
11 Gender-neutral possessive
12 Entertainment for general audiences?
13 Collection at the Musée d'Orsay
14 Nonactor with cameos in more than 20 Marvel movies
21 Playground comeback
23 ___ Fierce (onetime Beyoncé alter ego)
24 Certain grenade, for short
27 Batman?
29 "Neat-o-rific!"
31 Aquarium fish
33 People thinking on their feet?
35 Road sign silhouette
37 No-goodniks
38 Song that starts "Hate New York City / It's cold and it's damp"

39 Slowly picked up
40 Comeback
42 Battled
43 Model
44 Early Judaic sect
47 End
50 The Antichrist, with "the"
51 They may grab a bite
54 Lisbon lady
56 Beatles title girl with a "little white book"
58 Boring thing
59 Came down with

by Paolo Pasco

35

ACROSS

1 Social app with the slogan "the world's catalog of ideas"
10 City with the world's largest clock face
15 Hypnotized
16 Joan of Arc quality
17 Kale or quinoa, it's said
18 Phone charger feature
19 Father of Fear, in myth
20 Many sisters
22 This, in Taxco
23 A crane might hover over one
24 "Good thinking!"
26 Active ingredient in marijuana, for short
28 City in central Israel
29 Through
31 Place for bowlers
35 Ornamental garden installation
37 Quick tennis match
38 Part of a devil costume
39 Fuming
41 "You don't want to miss it!"
42 Bit of bronze
43 Statue outside Boston's TD Garden
44 Lunk
45 Watering holes
48 Eye-opening problem?
52 First name in gossip
53 Knee jerk, perhaps
55 Political accusation
56 Bill Clinton or George W. Bush, informally
58 Only highest-grossing film of the year that lost money
60 Stocking stuff
61 Spots that might smear
62 Pirouetting, perhaps
63 Bought or sold, e.g.

DOWN

1 Fibonacci, notably
2 Temper
3 Pickup points
4 Statistician's tool
5 Say irregardless?
6 Nickname for a two-time Wimbledon winner
7 State
8 Variety of quick bread
9 Multimedia think piece
10 Stephen Curry was one in '15 and '16
11 Like some seals
12 Feature of the 1876 or 2000 presidential election
13 Cup or bowl, but not a plate
14 2012 thriller with John Goodman and Alan Arkin
21 Straight men
25 Boobs
26 4.0, maybe
27 They're straight
30 Chick's tail?
31 Party person
32 Bacteriologist's discovery
33 What emo songs may convey
34 Org. doing pat-downs
36 "Tommyrot!"
40 Large letter in a manuscript
41 Hare-hunting hounds
46 Painter Veronese
47 European country whose flag features a George Cross
48 Relieve, in a way
49 Child of Uranus
50 Passing concern?
51 Off
52 Informal move
54 It's water under the bridge
57 Successful campaign sign
59 Cut of the pie chart: Abbr.

by Andrew Kingsley

36

ACROSS

1 Ultimate necessity
8 Needs grease, maybe
14 Cup holder
15 School whose mascot is Riptide the Pelican
16 Became untied
17 Intro to Comp Sci, for Data Structures, e.g.
18 Push away
19 Giant in sports entertainment
20 Made new?
21 Something you might take a pass on
22 Valuable diamond
24 Hosp. readout
25 Bigwig
28 One __ (multivitamin)
29 Highly sought-after things
31 Foucault's "This Is Not __"
32 This
36 Certain powerful engines, briefly
37 Warrants
38 Newswoman Burnett
39 Guiding light?
40 Writes to briefly?
43 Replies of understanding
44 Month with two natl. holidays
45 Auto name discontinued in 1986
48 One is a prize for scoring
50 Endowed with from the start, as money
52 Nobody special
53 Mace and shield, e.g.
54 Took for a ride
55 Hopeful
56 Closely following
57 Order that's rarely followed?

DOWN

1 Play
2 Fair, e.g.
3 Key
4 Gem
5 Place for a long run, maybe
6 Big __ Conference
7 Summer Olympics event
8 "A Prairie Home Companion" broadcast site
9 Becomes a traitor
10 "Where Is the Life That Late __?" ("Kiss Me, Kate" number)
11 One with connections to traveling speakers?
12 Largest sesamoid bones
13 Et __ (footnote abbr.)
14 Not one's best effort, in coachspeak
21 Ache
23 They can turn red in a flash
26 Contract employee?
27 Actor with the title role in "Robin Hood: Men in Tights"
28 Loan figs.
29 Beam
30 Some linemen: Abbr.
31 Just do it
32 Baseball exec Epstein
33 What to call Judge Judy
34 Words of longing
35 Some help from above
39 Southernmost city on I-35
40 Looms
41 Wolverine of Marvel Comics, e.g.
42 Derisive reaction
44 Reno, for one
46 They're not pros
47 Animal in un parc zoologique
49 Old "Red, White & You" sloganeer
50 Small nail
51 River to the Seine
52 "What you can get away with," according to Andy Warhol

by David Liben-Nowell

ACROSS

1 Really huge number
10 Bridge pair, briefly?
15 In a foreboding manner
16 Bane of cereal grain
17 Sufficiently good
18 Sauce often made with lemon juice
19 TiVo remote button
20 Not go to
21 Jerks
22 Lose, as a carrier might with a call
24 New York restaurateur with a Tony Award
26 Doomed
27 Round of four
29 B-ball
31 ___ Dolly ("Winter's Bone" heroine)
32 Contraction in Hamlet's soliloquy
34 1972 blaxploitation film with a soundtrack by Curtis Mayfield
36 Gun point?
40 Fur-lined cloak
41 Tight hold
43 A.L. or N.L. East: Abbr.
44 Some sports cars
45 Six-time U.S. Open champ
47 Get one's fill?
51 "That was exhausting!"
53 Ammonia and others
55 Longtime TV figure known for his garage
56 Dawgs
58 Liver by the Loire?
60 Sculptor who described art as "a fruit that grows in man"
61 "A Dog of Flanders" author
62 Bails
64 Beehive Blender brand
65 It fell in 2016 for the first time since 1919
66 Reviewers of scientific papers
67 Cause of rebellion, maybe

DOWN

1 Thanksgiving table decorations
2 A in physics class?
3 Adolescent program, slangily
4 Goddess who saved Odysseus
5 Records
6 Doesn't show oneself, say
7 So-called "Shakespeare of the Prophets"
8 Veterans
9 Host of the web series "Emoji Science"
10 Junior posthumously inducted into the Football Hall of Fame
11 Victorians
12 Searches for oneself
13 Mustard and others
14 Dirty look
21 Rewarded for waiting
23 Climber's aid
25 Decorate
28 Blacken a bit
30 Baseball commissioner during the steroid era
33 Robot arm movers
35 Navratilova, to 45-Across, e.g.
36 "Well, la-di-frickin'-da!"
37 It has big screens for small films
38 Apple operating system that's also a geographical name
39 One to one, say
42 Seemingly everywhere
46 ___ l'oeil
48 Hideous foe of Popeye
49 Strips, as a ship
50 Valve with a disc at the end of a vertically set stem
52 Like the Atlantic Ocean, slightly, from year to year
54 Barely drink
57 They may ring after parties
59 She, in Venice
62 Project
63 Stop: Abbr.

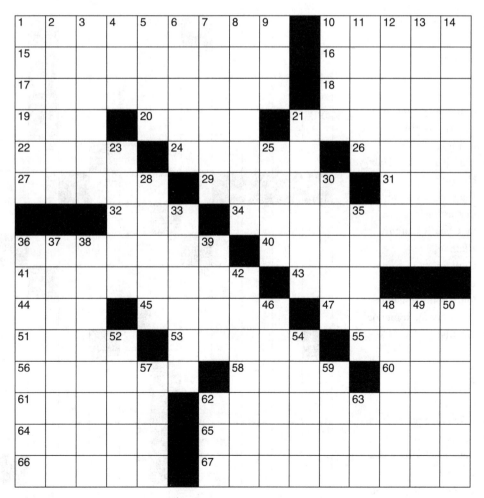

by Kristian House

38

ACROSS

1 Handle things
5 Try out
9 Additional
14 With nobody playing, say
16 Retro stereo component
17 Life preserver?
18 Katherine of NBC's "State of Affairs"
19 Observes closely
20 Girl adopted by Silas Marner
21 Anxious
22 Anti-___ League (Progressive Era organization)
24 Blade brand
26 On the program
28 Feels deep sympathy
32 Site of Oscar Wilde's trials
34 By and by
35 Sound effects pioneer Jack
36 Mandatory courses
37 Eponym of Bible history
39 Ehrich ___ a.k.a. Harry Houdini
40 Was unconsciously disturbing?
41 "I, Claudius" figure
43 Blathers
45 Component of some biodiesels
50 Ones coming ashore
51 Put away for someone
53 Drafted
54 One with changing needs
55 It may be off the charts
56 Like some physicians
57 Fuses
58 Person offering you a fortune
59 Command that a dog shouldn't follow

DOWN

1 Section of a botanical garden
2 School zone?
3 Top of the winter
4 Swords, in Sèvres
5 PC-linking program
6 It's hard to find in a crowd
7 8:00–9:00 on TV, e.g.
8 Proverbial certainty
9 Shakespeare character who coins the term "primrose path"
10 Winner of back-to-back Best Rock Instrumental Grammys in 1980 and 1981
11 The ordinary folk
12 "Scientists dream about doing great things. ___ do them": James A. Michener
13 Capacity
15 Gigli and pici, for two
23 "Dear ___" (1960s–'70s radio program)
25 Longtime "Voice of the New York Yankees"
27 Easter stock
28 Does some grilling
29 Quarters' quarters?
30 Group that almost can't fail?
31 Added to a plant
33 Treat with violent disrespect
35 Become dull
38 Lives the high life
39 Go downhill
42 Chicago Sun-Times columnist Richard
44 Soft options?
46 Brainy high school clique
47 Cosmic path
48 Former Trump Organization member
49 Like Ziegfeld girls
50 Thick of things, in a manner of speaking
52 Kid Cudi's "Day 'n' ___"

by Patrick Berry

ACROSS

1 One making waves over the waves
10 Bridge support
14 Lothario's activity
16 Wearing red to a Chinese funeral, e.g.
17 It has no life
19 Very well-pitched
20 Become flowery
21 Fat: Fr.
22 Cuff
23 Company that makes Tamiflu
24 Mailed or faxed
26 Head of Hogwarts
28 Salon job
30 Says "Top o' the morning," say
32 Shoshone language relative
33 Quite removed (from)
36 Manager honored at Cooperstown in 2013
40 Marker
41 Kitchen drawers?
43 Pilates class sights
45 Southern African game
46 Give a raise?
50 Zoom (along)
52 Many are named after M.L.K.
54 Sit (down) heavily
55 Bond femme fatale
57 Prestidigitator's word
58 Summoning statement
60 Cousin of a kite
61 Modern parents may try to limit it
62 Jazz combo?
63 Broadway star who was on Nixon's list of enemies

DOWN

1 Playground set
2 Painter Jean-___ Fragonard
3 Certain Cornhusker
4 Film setting?
5 Drawn together
6 "Huckleberry Finn" character
7 Conductor who has a hall at Tanglewood named after him
8 Worthy of reference
9 Lego competitor
10 Administer, as a shot
11 "The Consolation of Philosophy" author
12 Aeschylus, Sophocles and Aristophanes
13 College recruitment org.
15 Camera manufacturer whose slogan is "Be a Hero"
18 Shout of surprise
22 Genre that "The Long Goodbye" is based on
25 "Cake Boss" network
27 World capital with 40 islands within its city limits
29 Breakfast spot?
31 Cannon shot in Hollywood
33 Word shouted before "Fire!"
34 Material for mounting photos
35 Get perfectly pitched, in a way
37 Midwest college town
38 Farm butter
39 Openings in the computer field?
42 Longtime "Meet the Press" moderator
44 Places for pilots
45 Digs around
47 Cesario's lover in literature
48 Serious
49 Worked the field, in a way
51 "Yet that thy brazen gates of heaven may ___": Shak.
53 Pianist McCoy ___, member of the John Coltrane Quartet
55 Hearing command
56 Brief moments
57 Start of a classic boast
59 c, in a text

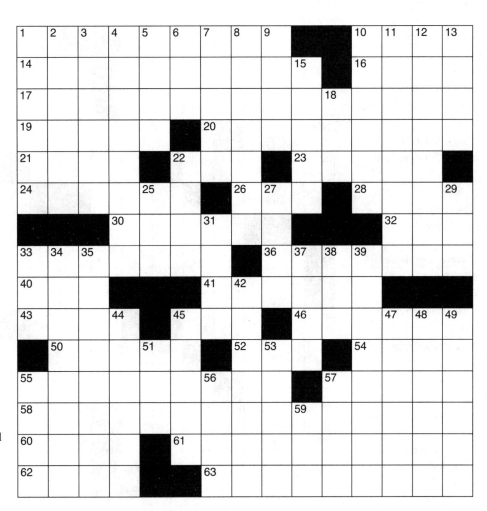

by Andrew Zhou

40

ACROSS

1 Golf handicap of zero
8 Like some garages
14 Where Forrest Gump played college football
15 Everything included
16 "Funky Cold Medina" rapper
17 Gives a walk-through, say
18 Fig. on a quarterly report
19 Test pattern?
21 Certain flight pattern
22 1970s TV spinoff
24 Some mouse cells
25 Broadway score?
26 Weigh station sight
27 Place to go when you're not going to the races, for short?
28 Joneses (for)
29 Creamy chilled soup
33 Source of break-dancing beats
35 N.B.A. M.V.P. who has hosted "Saturday Night Live"
36 Inroad
37 New Agey sounds
38 Facial option at a spa
42 "Everyone's private driver" sloganeer
43 Kind of walk
45 River of forgetfulness
46 Jerk
47 "The Chalk Garden" playwright, 1955
49 Shipload
50 1983 hit song that mentions Santa Monica Boulevard
52 Arcane matters
54 Lazy bum
55 Access
56 Playwright Eve
57 Pinch-hitter

DOWN

1 Figures in ribald Greek plays
2 Make a decent person out of?
3 Stochastic
4 Vigoda of "The Godfather"
5 Shire of "The Godfather"
6 "Get outta here!"
7 Collaborative computer coding event
8 Plants sometimes used to make flour
9 Letter of the law?
10 Not you specifically
11 Exchange words
12 Creature that Dalí walked on a leash in public
13 Puts back in the original state
15 Weapon that's thrown
20 Swedish-based maker of infant carriers
23 Seedy place to drink
25 "I'm down with that"
27 Quattuor doubled
28 Rip off
30 Reply that's a bit of a humblebrag
31 Contestants in a war of words?
32 BJ's competitor, informally
33 Major blood protein
34 Cry before taking the plunge
36 Pointless
39 Make it
40 What it always starts with?
41 College where Rutherford B. Hayes was valedictorian
43 Less tanned
44 "OMG!," old-style
45 Component of the combo drug Sinemet
47 Actress Daniels or Neuwirth
48 Practice exam?
51 ___ d'Isère (French ski resort)
53 Spam's place

by James Mulhern

ACROSS

1 Yoda, e.g.
11 Communication problem?
15 Last of a series of nicknames
16 Zero
17 Billy Crystal's role in "The Princess Bride"
18 Enigma machine decoder Turing
19 It's not a welcome sign
20 Facebook and others
21 Primary funding sources, briefly
22 Facebook, for one
23 Org. whose symbol is an eagle atop a key
24 How garden vegetables may be planted
26 Upset
28 Manicure destroyer
29 Hot Wheels garages?
33 Rhoda's TV mom
34 Emerald ___ borer
37 Expert savers
38 Constitution Hall grp.
39 Marathon champ Pippig
40 Mesozoic Era period
42 Home of Queen Margrethe II
44 Rank below marquis
47 "Let's do it!"
48 Sch. whose first building was Dallas Hall
51 Matches, at a table
53 "Caravan of Courage: An ___ Adventure" (1984 "Star Wars" spinoff)
54 Some Siouans
55 Bayh of Indiana politics
56 Flock gathering place
57 Group getting its kicks?
59 Rep
60 "I could use some help here . . ."
61 First name in architecture
62 Place to test the water

DOWN

1 Harry Potter's father
2 Alchemist's concoction
3 Frito-Lay chip
4 "Bleah!"
5 El Capitan platform
6 Literary hero whose name is Turkish for "lion"
7 Parts of a flight
8 2012 Republican National Convention host
9 Connection concerns, for short
10 "Toy Story" dino
11 Show impatience with
12 Developing company?
13 Wrapper that's hard to remove?
14 It's tailored to guys
24 Drinks with domed lids
25 Interest for a cryptozoologist
27 Impasse
28 Quadrant separator
30 "___ serious?"
31 Lab report?
32 Pay termination?
34 Nielsens measure
35 Fancy glasses
36 Malady with many "remedies"
41 Legal precedents
43 Get by
45 Awaken
46 Get support from
48 Photosynthesis opening
49 Interest of a mycologist
50 Quotidian
52 Old dummy
54 "Wait, I know that!"
57 Some savers' assets
58 Main hub for Virgin America, for short

by Robyn Weintraub

42

ACROSS

1 Connections
4 Connections to the sternum
8 Not assured at all
13 "You can figure as well as I can"
16 Treasure
17 Cream song with the lyric "Dance floor is like the sea, / Ceiling is the sky"
18 Things that may be compressed
19 Excluded category in the Paleo diet
20 Little treasure
21 Now
22 Kind of wave
23 Wasabi go-with in sushi meals
24 List heading
25 People who are in them are out, in brief
26 Shavit with the 2013 best seller "My Promised Land"
27 Where Spike Lee earned his M.F.A.
30 Little: Fr.
31 Not identifying with one's assigned sex
34 1851 Sojourner Truth speech
35 Online addresses, in part
36 "Ur hilarious!"
37 Bit of evasion
38 Still
39 Two or three sets, say
42 Where the Taj Mahotsav festival is held
44 Either director of "Inside Llewyn Davis"
46 Part of MSG
47 Fit
49 Info in a Yelp listing: Abbr.
50 Either half of a 1973 "duel"
51 Lacked options
52 Ask
54 Tribe whose name means "long tail"

55 Dessert so-called for its portions of flour, butter, eggs and sugar
56 Purchase at a golf pro shop
57 Purchases at a golf pro shop
58 Flushed

DOWN

1 "Don't you doubt me!"
2 "You cheated!"
3 Round containers?
4 Bet (on)
5 Subj. of many antiglobalization protests
6 Threat of a strike, in labor negotiations
7 Lead
8 Birdbrained
9 Birdbrain
10 Typical "S.N.L." start
11 Something you can control the volume with?
12 "Me?" follower
14 "___, boy!"
15 Terse and unadorned, as writing
23 Part of MGM's motto
26 "Babalú" bandleader
28 Ones ranking above knaves
29 Not realized
31 Fashion mogul Gunn
32 ___ Marcos, Tex.
33 Some "CSI" figs.
34 App with over 200 free stations

35 Place to play with toys
36 Things that might be batted at a ball
39 Approach
40 Something not many people laugh at
41 Blew it
43 Floral symbol of patience
45 ". . . but I could be wrong"
46 Comedian Maron
48 Superlatively
50 Contends (for)
53 Clément Marot poem "A ___ Damoyselle Malade"

by Natan Last

ACROSS

1 Ones making the rules?
16 "Thanks"
17 Passage between Sicily and the toe of Italy
18 Laughfests
19 Take home, perhaps?
20 ___ scripta (statutes)
21 Blyth of "Mildred Pierce"
22 Word before or after "what"
23 Org. opposed to weaving?
25 Scottish refusal
27 Band from the East
29 "1984" concern
38 Pre-buffet declaration
39 Take legal action, say
40 Sheep-counting times
41 Gendered Spanish suffix
42 Prize for Pizarro
43 Gulf War ally
46 Occasion for dragon dances
48 Cousin of a zebra
51 Something that might interrupt a flight, for short
53 "Little ___"
55 Frequent flier
57 Didn't mince words
60 It's of no concern to a usurer
61 Showed caution, in a way

DOWN

1 Perfume named for Baryshnikov
2 Shirley of "Goldfinger"
3 It comes with strings attached
4 Cross words
5 "Mila 18" novelist
6 Abbr. after many a military name
7 Twenty: Prefix
8 Faboo
9 Go, for one
10 Whistle blower?
11 Model X maker
12 "___ complicated"
13 Labor day highlight
14 Batman co-creator Bob
15 Memphis-based record label
22 Large beer mug
24 "Stay"
25 Ad follower?
26 Hopeless
28 Doesn't need a thing
29 Server's bread and butter
30 Round openings in domes
31 Shredded
32 French thinker?
33 Sounds during a massage
34 Arteries: Abbr.
35 Definitive disclaimer
36 Just slightly
37 Seas overseas
44 "Bird on ___" (Mel Gibson/Goldie Hawn comedy)
45 Picked up on
46 Tin anniversary
47 ___-deux
48 Fictional title character who declares "How puzzling all these changes are!"
49 Sub standard?
50 Way up
51 Hit the ground
52 Transparent sheet
54 More than more
55 Org. with many banned Super Bowl ads
56 "Before ___ you go . . ."
58 Clue follower: Abbr.
59 What's left on a farm?

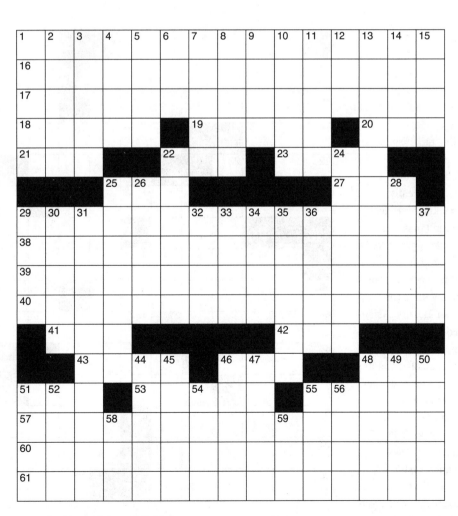

by Martin Ashwood-Smith

ACROSS

1 Like the national currency known as the tala
7 Axilla
13 "Hold on there now!"
15 Chasm
16 Powerful pitch
17 Settled with
18 London locale: Abbr.
19 Like the outer core of the earth
21 Certain logic gate
22 One Direction member Payne
24 The Flying Dutchman, e.g.
25 Limb-entangling weapon
26 One nearly cut Bond in half in "Goldfinger"
29 Rise up
30 1983 double-platinum album by Duran Duran
31 Everyday productivity enhancer, in modern lingo
33 Fictional character whose name is French for "flight of death"
36 Leading newspaper that took its name from a stage comedy
37 It's nothing, really
38 One making introductions
39 "You can't make me!"
44 Queen dowager of Jordan
45 Beyond repair
46 Ago, in an annual song
47 Animal with horns
48 Norman ___, first Asian-American to hold a cabinet post
50 Abbr. in an office address
51 Princess cake and others
53 Simply not done
56 Show disdain for, in a way
57 Subject of some PC Magazine reviews
58 Mixed forecasts?
59 N.F.L. Hall-of-Famer nicknamed "The Kansas Comet"

DOWN

1 Singer Twain
2 Blood lines
3 "Are you ___?!"
4 Cries that might be made while hopping on one foot
5 Slight interruption
6 Sure-to-succeed
7 One with commercial interests, for short
8 Nothing, in Nantes
9 Chant often heard toward the end of an N.B.A. season
10 Rick's, for one
11 Speech habits unique to an individual
12 The first one was delivered in 1984
13 "___ Stop the Rain" (1970 hit)
14 Fright night?
20 Pusillanimous
23 More festive
25 Views
27 Hiker's climb
28 Six-time Hugo Award winner Ben
29 Invoice word
32 Actress Sherilyn who was an Emmy nominee for "Twin Peaks"
33 Common ingredient in furniture polish
34 "No doubt!"
35 NASA spacecraft designed for travel to Mars
36 Units at a horse race
40 Whiskered animals
41 With 54-Down, longtime Long Island home of Theodore Roosevelt
42 Lays to rest
43 Frigid temps
45 They may have bullets
48 Main thrust
49 Field
52 The Nikkei 225 is one of its indexes: Abbr.
54 See 41-Down
55 Some lines of Milton

by Mary Lou Guizzo and Jeff Chen

ACROSS

1 Pot remnant
6 Pot part
10 Anagram of "pots"
14 Magnetic flux unit
15 Pot
17 Word from the Greek for "feigned ignorance"
18 Source of the word "geyser"
19 Professional boxer?
20 One who doesn't need fancy wining and dining
21 Prestigious award or flattering compliment
23 Talk like a pirate, say
24 Things short people have?
28 Open-house grp.
29 Make more powerful
34 Spill over
35 Spa treatment favored by rock fans?
38 Something no one can sing?
39 Senator who wrote "Why Courage Matters" and "Hard Call"
40 Sleazeball
41 Cutting edge producer
43 Certain tablets
45 Words from the speechless
50 "It's not only me who thinks this"
53 Fiscal __
56 Sway with a partner
57 BBC __
58 Serving of ahi
59 Beside
60 Azalea with the 2014 #1 hit "Fancy"
61 Fractions of fluid oz.
62 Off-color

DOWN

1 Exercise at the Y, maybe
2 Knight in shining armor
3 Solvent
4 Not follow suit
5 Process, in a way, as peanuts
6 Firenze friend
7 Sports bar bite
8 Joyce Kilmer poem that starts "I think that I shall never see"
9 Israeli seaport
10 Informal summer wear
11 Word of mock fanfare
12 Doing the job
13 Tempo
16 Said something in jest
22 One stuck in the closet
23 Full-bodied
25 "Deadly" vodka cocktail
26 Caesar dressing?
27 Hastened
28 Elite group of grads
30 N.C.A.A. hoops giant
31 Top part of a trunk, for short
32 Actress Thurman
33 Basic PC program
36 Nautical nuisance
37 Bright orange seafood delicacy
42 Settings for some Monet artwork
44 "What a knockout!"
46 One of the Earp brothers
47 Ache (for)
48 Take the top off
49 Tries to 54-Down
50 Freisa d'__ (Italian wine)
51 Bullet
52 King __
54 See 49-Down
55 Square type

by David Steinberg

ACROSS

1 Amphibian once associated with bad spirits
5 Big coverage provider
10 Nipper
14 No longer stuck on
15 ___ Motel
16 Crop circles, e.g.
17 Part of many a rural skyline
18 Line up
19 Former Soviet leader Andropov
20 Singer Goulding
22 Bad way to run
23 Start of some Southwest city names
24 Film title role for Tyrone Power and Brad Pitt
26 Theoretical
27 ___ Kosh B'Gosh
28 Wrigley's field
29 Noted bomb in a longtime war
31 Energy qtys.
33 Block letters?
35 Staying put
36 Skeptical rejoinder
39 Vegan milk source
41 "Sketches by ___" (1830s work)
42 Criticize in no uncertain terms
45 Ranchers' enemies
47 Dispensary measures: Abbr.
49 ___-cow
50 Civil engineering projects
51 One might take you in
54 Producer for Bowie and the Talking Heads
55 ___ sch.
56 French toast
57 Like Hawaiian shirts
59 Denver's ___ University
61 Place

62 Warranting a heart on Instagram, say
63 Bridge unit
64 Trochee's counterpart
65 Emperor after Galba
66 Flip
67 Father of Harmonia

DOWN

1 Hook remover, perhaps
2 Most baleful
3 "Huh, how about that!"
4 French crowd?
5 Only three-letter constellation other than Leo
6 Driver's visual aids in bad weather
7 West Coast N.F.L.'er
8 Certain blackjack
9 Basic order at Domino's
10 "Go ___ ways to a nunnery": Hamlet
11 Statement akin to "Have we met?"
12 Bar activity
13 Was
21 Headlines, for short?
25 Comeuppance
26 Fast-food debut of 1981
30 Turn tail?
32 Drives off
34 Hunky-dory
37 Sugar lover
38 Extended interview components

39 Big name in auto parts
40 Give for a while
43 "I messed up . . . what of it?!"
44 Jet settings
46 White of the eye
48 Yearbook div.
52 Backing
53 Actress Shire
58 "___ gratias"
60 Blue hue

by Damon Gulczynski

47

ACROSS

1 Instagram alternative
9 Smart
15 "Gentlemen, this is vodka" sloganeer
16 Melter on winter sidewalks
17 Checking locales
18 See 48-Across
19 Masago, at a sushi bar
21 Something well-kept?
22 Camp vehicle
25 Winged figure of myth
26 Bounds
27 Any day now
28 Thinking one is pretty hot stuff, say
29 Guy
30 Tech field, briefly
31 Blockheads?
35 Participant in the Battle of Saratoga, 1777
37 Subscription prescription
38 Hummer in the summer
40 All Saints' Day vis-à-vis All Souls' Day
41 1960 Pirates World Series hero, familiarly
42 "That was ___ . . ."
43 Hammer part
44 Pressure, informally
46 Whole lot of nothing
47 Takes turns in a casino
48 Official 18-Across of Utah
49 Shakespearean sister
51 Keep off the grid, say
53 Japanese import set in a kitchen
57 Charles Schwab alternative
58 Space in a paper available for journalism instead of ads
59 Stored (within)
60 25-Across, for one

DOWN

1 "___ Utah!" (state license plate slogan)
2 Big inits. in computing
3 Had dinner
4 Individual
5 Iceland has a cold one
6 Get an edge on
7 Flight preventer
8 Tryout
9 Total zoo
10 Driving range?
11 "The Greatest: My Own Story" author
12 Fox hunt leader of old
13 Conservative
14 RESPONDS LIKE THIS!
20 Five-in-a-row U.S. Open winner
22 Private stock
23 Sweetie
24 Detritus on New Year's morning
26 Maneuver carefully
28 Headline
29 "Buddenbrooks" novelist
31 ___ bath
32 Statistics class figure
33 Like the historic Battle of Lepanto, 1571
34 Mountains
36 "Beat it!"
39 Dressing down
43 Leader of five N.C.A.A. basketball championships for Duke, informally
44 Hunt for a film?
45 1%, say
46 Gave one's parole
47 Final step in cleaning
49 Up to ___
50 Lucius S. ___, hardware chain store eponym
52 Muscle used in pull-ups, briefly
54 Chopper
55 "A New World Record" grp., 1976
56 Had dinner

by Ian Livengood

48

ACROSS

1 2000s James Cameron cyberpunk/sci-fi series
10 Sting
14 Co-star of Greta Garbo in "Ninotchka"
15 Difficult treatment, informally
16 Interviewee in 2014's "The Interview"
17 Catnip and others
18 "The Da Vinci Code" priory
19 Online shopping button
21 Trattoria order
22 Variety of poker, briefly
23 French possessive
24 Émile Zola's "La __ humaine"
25 Financially secure
26 Rioting, e.g.
28 Troubles
29 Goes one step too far?
31 Class for model students?
32 "For sure"
33 "Look Sharp. Live Smart" sloganeer
38 200 at a 500
42 Some Windows products
43 Some Windows systems
44 Two-time mythological role for Anthony Hopkins
45 Final, e.g.
46 It's an honor to wear
48 Poker declaration
49 Home
51 Mouths to feed?
52 Temper
53 Families often share them
56 Second-generation Japanese-American
57 Athena's gift to Athens
58 It's got teeth
59 Ones getting passes

DOWN

1 Hägar creator Browne
2 Ouzo flavorer
3 Bash
4 Hall-of-Famer from the 1950s–'60s Celtics
5 Forever __ (Internet meme)
6 Photographer Goldin
7 One billion cycles per second
8 Learned
9 Three-time U.S. Open champ in the 1980s
10 "Let's Go" group, 1979
11 Changes at Standard & Poor's, say
12 Eisenhower and Nixon biographer Stephen
13 Some office notes
15 __ Chang, Harry Potter's onetime crush
20 Top-secret disguises?
21 Grp. of 300 people?
25 Bonn boulevard
27 Experience a minor crash?
30 Fake
31 Golden __
33 Burlesque show wear
34 She's "too cute to be a minute over 17" in a Chuck Berry song
35 46-Across wearer since 1952
36 Dresser
37 Commensurate
38 Public access channel, e.g.
39 Computer program that blocks viruses
40 Stella Artois or Beck's
41 __ alum
47 Legalese conjunction
48 Noted Guangzhou-born architect
50 __ gratia
54 GPS abbr.
55 French possessive

by David Phillips

ACROSS

1 Message accompanied by red lips
16 Like a hot mess
17 Where everything has been checked
18 F-, H- or I-, but not G-
19 Gets full
20 Hawaiian Tropic stat
21 Fourth-row Battleship position
22 Greek for "vapor"
23 Fela ___, Afrobeat music pioneer
24 He racked up 270 goals and 645 assists
25 Storied abductee
26 Mann of pop
27 How some things are washed
29 Wage ___
31 Somme buddy
32 Something to chew
33 Ledger sums
36 Opposite of cruel
39 Many a Netflix viewing session
40 Sporty auto options
42 Peak in the eurozone
44 Drought, poverty and such
45 "___ me!"
46 Gershon of "Rescue Me"
47 "___ you!"
48 Like some Pashto speakers
49 Enjoy in the moment
50 They're good for the long haul
53 Game with one round
54 Like many floor cleaners

DOWN

1 Saturday, in Seville
2 South Korean compact
3 Setting of "Abbott and Costello in the Foreign Legion"
4 Start at a terminal, say
5 Longoria with two Gold Gloves
6 U. wish?
7 Get a lock on, e.g.
8 Start of a Christmas carol
9 Pointer's statement
10 "___ the thing . . ."
11 Common blood type: Abbr.
12 1950s Reds star Ted, for short
13 "My guess is . . ."
14 Symbol of authority
15 Many an Instagram
22 Mountainside dwelling
23 A bit, informally
25 Bro
26 Wild callas, e.g.
28 Kicks back (with)
30 Some bra parts
33 Event in which 3:43:13 is the world record
34 Restrained, as a dog
35 He partnered with Bear in 1923
36 Means of branding
37 Lack of worldliness
38 Los Estados Unidos, en México
39 Light bite site
41 Form of yoga
43 Breaks down in class
45 Like dales, but not glens
46 Ancient medical researcher
48 Phone ___
49 Web content
51 It included Ga., La. and Va.
52 I.R.S. employee: Abbr.

by David Woolf

50

ACROSS
1 Call in the evening
5 Thunderous sound
9 Island group near Fiji
14 Heckelphone lookalike
15 Good eats
17 For which two heads are better than one?
18 Doing particularly well
19 Prefers charges against
20 Site of an annual British music festival
21 Take advantage of
23 Ben who played the Wizard in "Wicked"
24 Grocery quantity
25 Soul producer
26 Lose intensity
27 Judas never attained it
33 Setting for Hawthorne's "The Marble Faun"
34 Really affected
35 Pasta option
36 Four-hour tour features?
38 Roughly 1% of the earth's atmosphere
39 Oaf
40 Wild
41 Offensive opportunities
45 Procter & Gamble product line
47 Without trying
49 Bygone cracker brand
51 Increases risk and reward
52 Maker of PerformX sportswear
53 Gets very near
54 Eatery with scales
55 Steel brackets with two flanges
56 "You __ Me" (1957 R&B hit)
57 Fall location

DOWN
1 __ & Hobbies (eBay category)
2 1998 coming-of-age novel by Nick Hornby
3 Oscar Madison's weekly event
4 Attends to
5 Tool with a bezel
6 How a nocturne is often played
7 First high priest of the Israelites
8 Leave nothing to chance
9 2013 Sandra Bullock/ Melissa McCarthy comedy
10 Bid
11 Very sad turnout
12 Big ravine
13 Commercial manufacturers
16 British Open winner of 1971 and 1972
22 Fitting
24 Unadorned
25 Baby foxes
27 Adjective-forming suffix
28 Took a course?
29 Old baseball coverage?
30 In a union
31 Atmospheric problem
32 All washed up
34 Broadway chorus dancers, informally
37 Sub entries
38 Word with carpenter or weaver
40 Mean
41 Full of excitement
42 Easygoing
43 Arabian port that's home to Sinbad Island
44 Part taker
45 Pasta option
46 __ Chigurh ("No Country for Old Men" villain)
48 Lectern locale
50 Figure in the Ynglinga saga

by Patrick Berry

1

B	A	S	S	■	S	W	E	R	V	E	■	M	R	S
R	I	T	E	■	H	A	L	O	E	D	■	Y	E	W
O	R	D	E	R	A	R	O	U	N	D	■	W	V	A
W	H	E	N	I	M	S	I	X	T	Y	F	O	U	R
N	O	N	A	M	E	■	■	■	■	C	R	E	D	■
I	R	I	S	■	F	A	R	E	W	E	L	L	S	■
E	N	S	■	L	A	M	I	N	A	T	E	D	■	■
■	■	R	I	C	E	P	I	L	A	F	■	■	■	■
■	L	O	V	E	B	E	A	D	S	■	B	R	A	■
■	P	O	L	E	D	A	N	C	E	■	D	R	I	P
S	O	U	L	■	■	■	N	L	E	A	S	T	■	■
P	E	R	S	O	N	A	L	O	P	I	N	I	O	N
E	T	E	■	T	O	M	A	T	O	P	A	S	T	E
L	I	E	■	O	R	I	S	O	N	■	L	E	T	S
L	C	D	■	H	A	S	H	E	D	■	I	D	O	S

2

D	R	E	A	M	G	I	R	L	S	■	P	O	S	H
D	O	G	G	I	E	D	O	O	R	■	A	S	T	O
A	N	O	I	N	T	I	N	G	S	■	S	C	A	M
Y	A	N	N	I	■	D	D	S	■	S	T	A	R	E
■	■	C	O	S	M	O	■	S	H	O	R	T	O	■
■	P	H	O	N	E	Y	■	P	S	I	■	W	S	W
L	I	E	U	■	A	B	S	O	R	P	T	I	O	N
A	L	A	R	M	■	E	E	C	■	S	O	L	V	E
C	O	T	T	O	N	S	W	A	B	■	O	D	E	R
E	T	E	■	V	E	T	■	H	U	S	K	E	R	■
R	E	N	N	E	T	■	C	O	S	T	A	■	■	■
A	R	G	O	S	■	P	A	N	■	U	S	E	M	E
T	R	I	M	■	L	E	T	T	E	R	T	R	A	Y
E	O	N	S	■	B	R	E	A	K	D	A	N	C	E
D	R	E	G	■	J	E	R	S	E	Y	B	O	Y	S

3

P	A	W	N	■	S	T	E	A	L	T	H	I	E	R
E	P	E	E	■	W	A	L	L	A	W	A	L	L	A
R	E	N	O	■	I	N	M	E	M	O	R	I	A	M
U	N	C	L	O	G	S	■	■	R	A	T	S	■	■
■	N	E	A	P	■	■	Z	I	P	C	O	D	E	■
S	I	S	T	E	R	S	I	N	L	A	W	■	■	■
O	N	L	I	N	E	P	O	K	E	R	■	M	E	W
D	E	A	N	■	N	I	N	J	A	■	R	O	N	A
A	S	S	■	L	A	D	I	E	S	F	I	R	S	T
■	■	H	O	M	E	S	T	E	A	D	A	C	T	■
■	P	R	E	T	E	R	M	■	■	V	E	T	O	■
A	R	A	L	■	■	■	S	E	A	S	O	N	S	■
W	I	N	E	S	E	L	L	E	R	■	O	R	C	A
O	Z	O	N	E	L	A	Y	E	R	■	F	I	E	F
L	E	N	S	C	O	V	E	R	S	■	F	A	D	E

4

A	S	T	R	I	D	■	■	G	E	T	S	A	T	■
S	W	E	E	P	E	A	■	C	L	A	R	I	C	E
C	A	S	T	O	F	T	H	O	U	S	A	N	D	S
O	T	S	■	D	E	R	A	L	T	E	■	K	E	L
T	H	E	N	■	N	O	I	S	E	■	I	S	L	A
S	E	R	A	■	S	I	T	O	N	■	S	I	C	S
■	■	D	A	N	T	E	S	I	N	F	E	R	N	O
■	■	■	E	V	A	■	■	R	E	A	■	■	■	■
■	P	O	T	A	T	O	P	E	E	L	E	R	S	■
S	E	N	T	■	T	R	A	D	E	■	L	A	T	E
K	N	E	E	■	O	N	T	A	P	■	I	T	A	L
I	T	O	■	F	R	A	C	T	A	L	■	E	N	D
B	A	C	K	I	N	T	H	E	S	A	D	D	L	E
I	N	A	T	R	E	E	■	S	T	R	I	P	E	R
B	E	T	S	E	Y	■	■	A	D	A	G	E	S	■

5

I	M	U	P	■	B	L	I	G	E	■	C	A	S	T
N	A	N	O	■	O	U	T	E	R	■	A	C	H	Y
S	U	N	T	A	N	N	I	N	G	■	K	C	A	L
O	N	E	P	L	E	A	S	E	■	P	E	E	V	E
L	A	R	I	A	T	■	D	R	P	E	P	P	E	R
E	L	V	E	S	■	B	E	A	R	C	A	T	S	■
N	O	E	S	■	M	A	C	L	E	A	N	■	■	■
T	A	D	■	D	E	N	I	Z	E	N	■	P	T	A
■	■	C	E	L	A	D	O	N	■	B	A	R	R	■
■	L	E	A	V	E	N	E	D	■	R	O	R	E	M
W	E	L	L	R	E	A	D	■	S	E	R	V	E	R
U	N	I	T	Y	■	B	L	O	N	D	E	A	L	E
R	A	T	E	■	T	O	Y	P	O	O	D	L	E	S
S	P	E	C	■	B	A	S	E	R	■	O	U	S	T
T	E	S	H	■	S	T	O	N	E	■	M	E	S	S

6

G	A	W	P	■	O	D	I	C	■	U	N	G	E	R
A	C	H	E	■	H	O	R	A	■	N	A	O	M	I
G	R	A	N	D	S	T	A	N	D	S	E	A	T	S
A	E	T	N	A	■	S	E	N	A	T	■	T	S	K
■	M	E	R	C	■	■	E	N	O	L	A	■	■	■
A	M	O	D	E	S	T	P	R	O	P	O	S	A	L
M	A	R	■	D	I	A	R	Y	■	S	O	N	D	E
P	R	E	V	■	S	K	I	R	T	■	N	A	D	A
A	S	C	I	I	■	E	M	O	R	Y	■	I	L	K
S	H	A	I	L	E	N	E	W	O	O	D	L	E	Y
■	N	I	L	L	A	■	■	U	K	E	S	■	■	■
A	N	I	■	B	E	B	O	P	■	E	X	P	A	T
J	E	S	S	I	C	A	C	H	A	S	T	A	I	N
A	B	A	F	T	■	C	H	I	N	■	E	C	R	U
R	O	Y	C	E	■	K	O	L	N	■	R	E	S	T

7

LOCAVORE / HIPPO
LOADEDUP / AENEID
ALSORANS / NEATLY
MOI / BYE / GODDESS
ANNE / LOU / ARES
GOLDILOCKSZONE
MIDAIR / KESEY
AST / DAB / ALI / ERS
CORDS / OOZING
CRYYOUREYESOUT
ICAN / HED / ORES
DECATUR / MBA / BEN
ERASER / HEATWAVE
NESTEA / ONEOWNER
TREYS / BUZZFEED

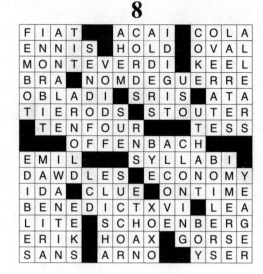

8

FIAT / ACAI / COLA
ENNIS / HOLD / OVAL
MONTEVERDI / KEEL
BRA / NOMDEGUERRE
OBLADI / SRIS / ATA
TIERODS / STOUTER
TENFOUR / TESS
OFFENBACH
EMIL / SYLLABI
DAWDLES / ECONOMY
IDA / CLUE / ONTIME
BENEDICTXVI / LEA
LITE / SCHOENBERG
ERIK / HOAX / GORSE
SANS / ARNO / YSER

9

CAPEFEAR / NEWTOY
ALOELACE / OXHIDE
VAMOOSED / TAILOR
EMP / RES / GOMPERS
BOOMED / JURIS
ADULT / GEMINIS
TOSS / BETWEENUS
SMA / PENSETS / RIG
ESCAPEKEY / FETA
SUBARID / LOYAL
TATAS / ROBOTO
NOSTRIL / BOA / UHS
IMLIKE / SANDRAOH
SEAMEN / OHDEARME
INVERT / USERFEES

10

BED / ABDULJABBAR
RPI / CARTOONLIKE
OHS / CHEERLEADER
WEPT / RISES / BELA
MARTA / NOG / NAN
PERIWIGS / NAB
DRACONIAN / SEPTA
FATES / FHA / KAROL
SLEPT / TITLEROLE
SET / BLOTCHES
ZAC / PAD / USAIR
EDOM / IRANI / TBAR
RADIOLOGIST / IBO
ONETWOPUNCH / TLC
GARTERSNAKE / SEA

11

RASHAD / LACERATE
EZPASSTOLLLANES
HEAVYCASUALTIES
ARMEE / BSIDES
BAS / ABO / PGA
TAKEFORAFOOL
FEMININEWILES
BARITONESAXES
MOUNTAINBIKER
THREESTOOGES
ARE / CTN / TAG
OMELET / OSAGE
AMERICANLARCHES
MADECONCESSIONS
PAULKLEE / LOSETO

12

MINICAR / STRAFE
ONTHEMAP / IBANEZ
IDEALIZE / TANGLE
RUST / RENOIR / ELK
ESTEE / CNN / ELOI
LAVIE / CREPE
TRAVELCHANNEL
LESTERPEARSON
SILVERBULLETS
PEEPS / OSLER
YAPS / ASH / SOSAD
WHO / GREENS / HOLY
AERIAL / ROEVWADE
RATTLE / STEWOVER
EDSELS / ANSWERS

13

P	E	N	P	A	L	■	S	L	O	W	J	A	M
A	V	I	A	T	E	■	S	T	O	N	E	A	G	E
C	E	L	L	O	S	■	P	A	P	E	R	C	U	T
K	N	E	E	L	■	H	A	T	S	■	E	K	E	S
■	A	L	S	A	C	E	■	P	O	L	■
H	A	L	L	■	T	I	E	S	■	I	N	E	P	T
O	B	I	E	■	A	R	R	A	N	T	■	M	O	A
H	A	N	S	O	L	O	■	V	I	T	A	M	I	N
U	S	E	■	R	E	F	L	E	X	■	B	O	N	G
M	E	R	G	E	■	T	O	N	E	■	U	N	T	O
■	N	A	S	■	H	O	U	S	E	D	■
O	D	O	R	■	R	E	N	E	■	S	H	E	E	T
H	A	T	E	R	A	D	E	■	S	T	A	B	L	E
O	D	E	T	O	J	O	Y	■	P	E	B	B	L	E
H	A	S	H	T	A	G	■	A	R	I	S	E	N

14

O	R	A	L	B	■	S	O	F	T	■	M	O	A	T
D	O	P	E	R	■	C	L	O	I	S	O	N	N	E
D	U	E	T	O	B	U	D	G	E	T	C	U	T	S
S	E	D	U	C	E	D	■	G	R	A	S	S	E	S
■	P	A	L	■	Y	A	Y	■
U	S	S	■	D	O	G	S	■	C	A	S	A	B	A
T	H	E	N	E	W	Y	O	R	K	T	I	M	E	S
I	O	N	A	■	R	A	E	■	T	A	R	P
C	R	O	S	S	W	O	R	D	P	U	Z	Z	L	E
A	E	R	A	T	E	■	S	O	U	P	■	E	E	N
■	A	B	C	■	R	R	S	■
A	N	O	S	M	I	A	■	R	I	O	T	A	C	T
W	I	L	L	E	N	D	T	O	M	O	R	R	O	W
O	C	E	A	N	A	R	I	A	■	T	A	E	B	O
L	E	S	T	■	R	E	A	M	■	S	W	A	B	S

15

B	A	D	D	A	Y	■	L	A	P	C	A	T
O	T	O	O	L	E	■	T	E	A	R	O	S	E
N	A	U	S	E	A	■	F	U	N	H	O	U	S	E
A	N	G	E	R	■	S	A	R	A	■	B	R	U	T
M	E	H	■	T	A	P	I	N	■	K	E	T	C	H
I	N	N	S	■	W	A	T	S	O	N	■	S	H	E
■	D	U	N	C	A	N	H	I	N	E	S	■
■	T	A	L	K	I	N	G	H	E	A	D	■
■	G	O	E	S	O	N	A	D	I	E	T	■
A	I	R	■	A	S	H	M	A	N	■	D	A	R	K
S	P	E	A	K	■	M	O	L	D	S	■	D	I	E
K	H	A	N	■	P	A	R	S	■	H	O	B	B	Y
F	O	R	T	E	R	I	E	■	F	I	R	E	U	P
O	N	E	I	R	O	N	■	A	R	C	A	N	A
R	E	D	C	A	P	■	X	R	A	T	E	D

16

F	A	L	S	I	E	S	■	B	A	R	T	A	B	S
I	S	A	I	D	N	O	■	E	X	U	R	B	A	N
G	U	Y	C	O	D	E	■	L	O	S	E	S	T	O
T	S	E	■	L	O	V	E	I	N	S	■	O	R	R
R	U	T	H	■	R	E	Y	E	S	■	B	L	O	T
E	A	T	A	T	■	R	E	B	■	T	A	U	P	E
E	L	E	V	E	N	■	D	E	S	I	S	T	E	D
■	E	N	I	D	■	R	I	M	S	■
C	H	A	N	D	L	E	R	■	R	E	S	E	A	L
H	A	L	O	S	■	R	A	H	■	D	A	R	L	A
E	M	I	T	■	T	R	I	O	S	■	X	R	A	Y
W	B	A	■	C	H	I	L	L	A	X	■	A	M	O
T	O	S	P	A	R	E	■	D	U	B	S	T	E	P
O	N	E	O	V	E	R	■	E	C	O	C	I	D	E
Y	E	S	I	S	E	E	■	M	E	X	I	C	A	N

17

S	M	A	R	T	Y	P	A	N	T	S	■	G	P	A
M	A	D	E	Y	O	U	L	O	O	K	■	R	A	M
O	R	D	E	R	O	N	L	I	N	E	■	E	S	P
T	I	T	L	E	■	E	D	G	I	N	E	S	S
E	N	O	S	■	R	A	R	E	■	N	E	N	E
■	C	O	N	G	A	■	P	E	D	I
B	I	R	T	H	D	A	Y	■	D	R	A	G	O	N
O	V	A	R	I	E	S	■	N	A	I	L	G	U	N
Z	Y	D	E	C	O	■	S	O	L	O	I	S	T	S
O	L	I	N	■	W	I	L	E	S	■
■	E	A	C	H	■	A	N	O	S	■	P	U	M	A
C	A	T	H	O	L	I	C	■	F	I	N	E	R
A	G	O	■	L	I	V	E	A	L	I	T	T	L	E
F	U	R	■	E	M	E	R	G	E	N	C	I	E	S
E	E	S	■	S	P	R	E	A	D	S	H	E	E	T

18

F	I	V	E	A	M	■	J	E	T	B	L	A	C	K
A	C	A	D	I	A	■	I	N	R	E	A	S	O	N
B	Y	L	I	N	E	■	G	O	O	D	T	I	M	E
■	S	U	E	T	■	S	U	P	■	I	D	E	A
S	T	E	■	I	D	T	A	G	■	S	N	E	R	D
H	A	M	S	T	E	R	W	H	E	E	L	■
O	R	E	L	■	L	E	S	■	T	R	O	V	E
P	E	N	A	L	T	Y	■	H	E	A	V	I	N	G
■	S	U	M	M	A	■	F	O	R	■	E	R	G	O
■	P	A	S	S	I	O	N	F	R	U	I	T
T	A	B	O	O	■	U	N	D	E	R	■	S	N	O
A	L	O	E	■	S	N	L	■	E	A	S	E	■
S	O	R	T	D	A	T	A	■	T	E	R	C	E	T
T	H	E	R	A	V	E	N	■	S	T	M	A	R	K
E	A	S	Y	R	E	A	D	■	E	V	E	N	S	O

19

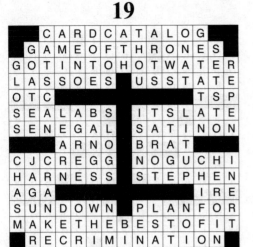

```
CARDCATALOG
GAMEOFTHRONES
GOTINTOHOTWATER
LASSOES  USSTATE
OTC          TSP
SEALABS  ITSLATE
SENEGAL  SATINON
    ARNO BRAT
CJCREGG  NOGUCHI
HARNESS  STEPHEN
AGA          IRE
SUNDOWN  PLANFOR
MAKETHEBESTOFIT
RECRIMINATION
DOAGOODTURN
```

20

```
PAJAMABOTTOMS
IMAGINEDRAGONS
VANESSAWILLIAMS
EZINE   ABLE  RAT
NEED  SPLAYS  ERE
      APPALL  HDTV
SAG  ARIA  FIERCE
ETERNAL  SICHUAN
ATTEST  CORE  MRS
GABS   TRUSTS
RCA  TSHIRT  PRIG
AKC  ATOM   CRUDE
MAKEMINEADOUBLE
DATINGAGENCIES
TALKSNONSENSE
```

21

```
ROGERTHAT  BOTCH
AROMARAMA  ACHOO
REFUSENIK  RHETT
EGO  HAG  EMERGES
GARBED  BOA  EIRE
ANTIS  FONDA  RIA
SOHN  ITO  OUTLET
   EGGMCMUFFIN
ANJOUS  BFF  TENK
SOU  MAGOO  MIXIN
PUGS  FAX  COSTCO
ERUPTED  MEN  DEC
CILIA  GUESTBOOK
TSARS  EARTHTONE
SHREK  TREASURED
```

22

```
SCRAMBLES  HAWED
WHATAJERK  OVATE
MANICOTTI  TAXON
   LARSEN  MIENS
BARTOK  FUELS
AME    GILLS  PET
RIAL  LENINSTOMB
OGLE  ERICA  DEBI
NOTAGBACKS  STAR
SSR  ROLES   IND
  ONEND  SHOCKS
BLOAT  FATTEN
LAPAZ  OPIONEERS
ALECK  RICOCASEK
HARPY  DESDEMONA
```

23

```
SCAGGS   SCALPS
CAPULET  ALCOTT
AVENUEB  MARACA
MERCEDES  PETRI
PACO  YANG  SHUN
STUNT  MART  SIL
   TIC  CABOOSE
SHERLOCKHOLMES
COLONELSANDERS
ONELOVE  MEH
FOG  WARS  SINEW
FRAT  LIES  COLE
LANES  CRACKPOT
ARTLAB  FLOORIT
WILLDO  SUCROSE
SAYYES   DAYBED
```

24

```
NEOPETS  CAUCUSED
EMPERORPALPATINE
BATTLEOFTHESEXES
UNITE  ININK  IMS
LACY  LIZARD  BRIE
ATAT  INEPT  WOOER
EELY  ERRS  MAINST
  RAGE   GIRL
ESTATE  BEAR  EWES
BORNE  TABLE  RASP
OMIT  BYROAD  MISO
NER  TURBO  OATEN
IHEARYOUKNOCKING
COMPOUNDSENTENCE
SWEETPEA  GEORGES
```

25

```
E S P N R A D I O ■ T E B O W
S T O N E C O L D ■ E M O T E
T A K E S H O L D ■ R I O T S
A T E ■ T O M B ■ K I T K A T
D I A N ■ O S I R I S ■ S W E
O C T E T ■ T I M ■ A C A N
■ V O I C E C O M M A N D
■ C O A R S E ■ O N I O N S ■
W I N D O W S P H O N E ■
R A S A ■ E A R ■ T B A R S
A B C ■ N A R I T A ■ A S H E
P A R L O R ■ M O D S ■ S O N
S T E A K ■ C A R D I G A N S
U T E R I ■ A T M I N S I D E
P A N D A ■ B E E T S A L A D
```

26

```
B L A D E S ■ Y U L E L O G
R E G I N A ■ F I R E L A N E
E G G N O G ■ R E A W O K E N
W A R E S ■ B E L L ■ E M T
S L E D ■ L A I D ■ O V A L
U P S ■ G A N G ■ S A L I N E
P A S S E D T H E T I M E ■
■ D O N T L E T M E D O W N
■ R O B E R T P R E S T O N
A N N O Y S ■ R I N D ■ E V A
M E A T ■ B A R E ■ P R E Y
S A T ■ B R I E ■ W O R M S
T R I A L R U N ■ C A S A B A
E T O N I A N S ■ P R I C E Y
L O N G E S T ■ A S T E R S
```

27

```
T A T T L E ■ F L A S H E R S
O N E M A N ■ A I R W O M A N
T A X C U T ■ N A G A S A K I
E P A ■ D E S T R O Y ■ J E T
B O S S ■ R I A L S ■ L O I S
A L B U M ■ C S I ■ M O R N
G I B L E T ■ Y A Z O O ■
■ S Q U A R E B R A C K E T ■
■ S T U P A ■ C H O R A L
■ F I E S ■ I S O ■ A U D I O
R I M A ■ A D E P T ■ T O L L
E G O ■ D O U B T I T ■ C G I
C A N B E R R A ■ L E S T A T
O R I E N T A L ■ L A K O T A
N O T A T A L L ■ S T A R E S
```

28

```
B L A C K F R I D A Y ■ T A B
T I T A N I U M O R E ■ A S U
W A I T I N G A R E A ■ K H Z
O R T ■ T A S M A N ■ G E E Z
■ M S G ■ G A T O S ■
A G R A ■ L A S ■ S U B L E T
T R A N S E P T S ■ R E E S E
B E D A N D B R E A K F A S T
A B A S E ■ S I G N S O V E R
T E R S E R ■ P O T ■ R E N A
■ B A R E R ■ I C E ■
P A L S ■ S A W Y E R ■ H A G
A M I ■ W I N E S T E W A R D
I M P ■ A N D R E A D O R I A
D O S ■ C Y B E R M O N D A Y
```

29

```
G R E A S Y ■ A F R I C A N S
L A U R I E ■ R A I L E D A T
A N G O R A ■ A L L I N D I A
C H E M I S T ■ L E A S E R S
I O N A ■ T A P E ■ D O D O S
A M I S S ■ B E N D ■ R O B E
L E E ■ I S O N ■ O P E N I N
■ U N I O N I Z E D ■
L E R N E R ■ A C E S ■ P C S
A X E S ■ E I N E ■ T A R O T
C A S E S ■ S T U B ■ D E V O
E M P T I E S ■ P L U M B E R
D I E T D R U G ■ O P I A T E
U N C L E L E O ■ T U R K E Y
P E T E B E S T ■ S P E E D S
```

30

```
J A G S ■ A D M ■ P A S T O R
A G R A ■ R E A ■ A D H E R E
P I E D ■ I N K S T A I N E D
A L A ■ S A T I E ■ M E T O O
N E T ■ E L E N I ■ A S H ■
■ B O A ■ G N P ■ O I L
A M A S S E D A F O R T U N E
H U R R I C A N E S E A S O N
A F R I C A N E L E P H A N T
S T I C K S A N D S T O N E S
H I E ■ H I T ■ I E D ■
■ R P M ■ D R A W L ■ Y E P
P A R E E ■ E A P O E ■ E G O
L E E K R A S N E R ■ J A R S
A R E O L A ■ C A D ■ O R E S
N O F E E S ■ E R Y ■ E S T E
```

31

F	O	G	S		S	C	A	T		A	T	A	L	L
I	N	R	I		P	O	O	H		M	O	X	I	E
T	E	A	C	H	A	B	L	E	M	O	M	E	N	T
S	P	Y	K	I	D	S			B	A	U	B	L	E	S
	E	M	O	T	E		C	E	R	N				
B	R	A	S	I		C	H	E	S	T	H	A	I	R
A	C	T		T	H	O	U	G	H		A	N	N	A
S	E	T	S		A	G	R	E	E		H	G	T	V
K	N	E	E		N	I	C	E	S	T		L	E	E
S	T	R	E	N	G	T	H	S		O	D	O	R	S
		O	D	A	Y		P	R	E	P	S			
I	N	K	B	L	O	T		Q	U	I	C	H	E	S
B	I	O	L	O	G	I	C	A	L	C	L	O	C	K
I	G	L	O	O		N	E	I	L		A	N	T	I
S	H	A	C	K		G	O	D	S		W	E	S	T

32

H	O	T	W	A	R	S		L	E	C	T	U	R	E
I	N	O	R	B	I	T		E	X	U	R	B	I	A
D	E	M	I	L	L	E		S	P	L	E	E	N	S
			T	E	E	N	J	E	O	P	A	R	D	Y
R	A	S	H		D	O	E		R	A	S			
A	R	C	E	D		S	L	A	T		O	A	H	U
P	E	R	S	O	N		L	I	T	A	N	I	E	S
C	T	A		J	U	D	O	M	A	T		R	I	A
D	O	W	J	O	N	E	S		X	A	N	A	D	U
S	O	L	I		C	A	H	N		D	U	C	E	S
		G	A	H		O	O	H		L	E	N	A	
F	L	A	G	R	A	N	T	F	O	U	L			
R	U	G	L	I	K	E		A	R	T	S	A	L	E
E	P	H	E	S	U	S		I	S	E	E	N	O	W
D	E	A	D	E	S	T		R	E	P	T	I	L	E

33

P	E	T	U	N	I	A	P	I	G		A	S	A	P
S	H	A	K	E	N	B	A	K	E		G	I	L	L
S	U	P	E	R	D	U	P	E	R		E	C	T	O
T	D	S		V	E	T	S			I	N	K	E	Y
		S	O	B	S			S	S	T	A	R	S	
S	P	R	O	U	T		P	I	A	N	O	S		
P	O	O	F	S		D	I	C	K	T	R	A	C	Y
A	L	O	T		V	E	X	E	S		A	D	O	S
N	E	T	P	R	O	F	I	T		I	N	O	N	E
	A	R	O	U	S	E		J	I	G	G	E	R	
A	G	R	E	E	S		D	A	N	E				
C	O	O	T	S		J	A	M	S		T	A	G	
C	R	U	Z		A	B	O	V	E	I	T	A	L	L
R	E	N	E		R	O	T	I	S	S	E	R	I	E
A	D	D	L		P	O	S	T	I	T	N	O	T	E

34

W	H	A	T	S	T	H	A	T		H	O	U	R	S
R	I	C	E	A	R	O	N	I		I	N	S	E	T
E	S	T	A	T	E	T	A	X		L	E	O	N	A
S	T	E	M		N	A	G		A	L	S	T	O	N
T	O	D		S	T	I	R	F	R	Y		O	I	L
E	R	I	C	A		R	A	R	E		S	U	R	E
D	Y	N	A	S	T		M	A	N	P	U	R	S	E
	S	H	E	D		G	O	O	P					
B	I	G	E	A	T	E	R		T	E	E	H	E	E
A	L	L	Y		R	E	E	D		T	R	A	P	S
D	O	E		B	A	R	B	E	T	S		D	I	S
E	V	A	D	E	S		I	M	O		R	A	T	E
G	E	N	O	A		B	R	I	N	G	I	T	O	N
G	L	E	N	S		I	T	S	G	O	T	I	M	E
S	A	D	A	T		T	H	E	S	T	A	T	E	S

35

P	I	N	T	E	R	E	S	T		M	E	C	C	A
I	N	A	T	R	A	N	C	E		V	A	L	O	R
S	U	P	E	R	F	O	O	D		P	R	O	N	G
A	R	E	S		A	U	N	T	S		E	S	T	O
N	E	S	T			N	E	A	T	I	D	E	A	
			T	H	C		L	O	D		V	I	A	
H	A	T	T	R	E	E		K	O	I	P	O	N	D
O	N	E	S	E	T			G	O	A	T	E	E	
S	T	E	A	M	E	D		B	E	T	H	E	R	E
T	I	N		O	R	R		A	S	S				
	T	A	P	R	O	O	M	S			S	T	Y	E
R	O	N	A		S	P	A	S	M		L	I	A	R
E	X	G	O	V		C	L	E	O	P	A	T	R	A
L	I	S	L	E		A	T	T	A	C	K	A	D	S
O	N	T	O	E		P	A	S	T	T	E	N	S	E

36

	F	R	I	S	B	E	E		S	T	I	C	K	S
B	R	A	S	T	R	A	P		T	U	L	A	N	E
G	O	T	L	O	O	S	E		P	R	E	R	E	Q
A	L	I	E	N	A	T	E		A	N	D	R	E	
M	I	N	T	E	D		B	U	S		A	C	E	
E	C	G		W	H	E	E	L		A	D	A	Y	
		G	R	A	I	L	S		A	P	I	P	E	
T	H	I	R	T	Y	T	W	O	A	C	R	O	S	S
H	E	M	I	S		M	E	R	I	T	S			
E	R	I	N		L	A	S	E	R			I	M	S
O	H	S		J	A	N			D	A	T	S	U	N
	O	S	C	A	R		B	O	R	N	I	N	T	O
A	N	Y	O	N	E		R	I	O	T	G	E	A	R
R	O	O	K	E	D		A	S	P	I	R	A	N	T
T	R	U	E	T	O		D	E	S	S	E	R	T	

37

G	A	Z	I	L	L	I	O	N	■	S	P	E	C	S
O	M	I	N	O	U	S	L	Y	■	E	R	G	O	T
U	P	T	O	G	R	A	D	E	■	A	I	O	L	I
R	E	C	■	S	K	I	P	■	T	U	G	S	O	N
D	R	O	P	■	S	A	R	D	I	■	S	U	N	K
S	E	M	I	S	■	H	O	O	P	S	■	R	E	E
■	■	T	I	S	■	S	U	P	E	R	F	L	Y	■
B	A	Y	O	N	E	T	■	P	E	L	I	S	S	E
I	R	O	N	G	R	I	P	■	D	I	V	■	■	■
G	T	S	■	E	V	E	R	T	■	G	A	S	U	P
W	H	E	W	■	O	D	O	R	S	■	L	E	N	O
H	O	M	I	E	S	■	F	O	I	E	■	A	R	P
O	U	I	D	A	■	J	U	M	P	S	S	H	I	P
O	S	T	E	R	■	U	S	P	O	S	T	A	G	E
P	E	E	R	S	■	T	E	E	N	A	N	G	S	T

38

C	O	P	E	■	T	E	S	T	■	O	T	H	E	R
A	C	A	P	P	E	L	L	A	■	P	H	O	N	O
C	E	R	E	A	L	B	O	X	■	H	E	I	G	L
T	A	K	E	S	N	O	T	E	■	E	P	P	I	E
I	N	A	S	T	E	W	■	S	A	L	O	O	N	■
■	■	■	A	T	R	A	■	B	I	L	L	E	D	■
A	C	H	E	S	■	O	L	D	B	A	I	L	E	Y
S	O	O	N	■	F	O	L	E	Y	■	C	O	R	E
K	I	N	G	J	A	M	E	S	■	W	E	I	S	S
S	N	O	R	E	D	■	N	E	R	O	■	■	■	■
■	P	R	A	T	E	S	■	C	O	R	N	O	I	L
S	U	R	F	S	■	O	N	R	E	S	E	R	V	E
W	R	O	T	E	■	D	I	A	P	E	R	B	A	G
I	S	L	E	T	■	A	T	T	E	N	D	I	N	G
M	E	L	D	S	■	S	E	E	R	■	S	T	A	Y

39

S	H	O	C	K	J	O	C	K	■	I	B	A	R	■
W	O	M	A	N	I	Z	I	N	G	■	N	O	N	O
I	N	A	N	I	M	A	T	E	O	B	J	E	C	T
N	O	H	I	T	■	W	A	X	P	O	E	T	I	C
G	R	A	S	■	N	A	B	■	R	O	C	H	E	■
S	E	N	T	T	O	■	L	O	O	■	T	I	N	T
■	■	E	L	I	D	E	S	■	U	T	E	■	■	■
A	F	A	R	C	R	Y	■	L	A	R	U	S	S	A
I	O	U	■	A	R	O	M	A	S	■	■	■	■	■
M	A	T	S	■	G	N	U	■	E	M	B	O	S	S
■	M	O	T	O	R	■	S	T	S	■	P	L	O	P
O	C	T	O	P	U	S	S	Y	■	V	O	I	L	A
Y	O	U	V	E	B	E	E	N	S	E	R	V	E	D
E	R	N	E	■	S	C	R	E	E	N	T	I	M	E
Z	E	E	S	■	S	T	R	E	I	S	A	N	D	■

40

S	C	R	A	T	C	H	■	T	W	O	C	A	R	■
A	L	A	B	A	M	A	■	B	A	R	N	O	N	E
T	O	N	E	L	O	C	■	O	R	I	E	N	T	S
Y	T	D	■	I	N	K	B	L	O	T	■	V	E	E
R	H	O	D	A	■	A	A	A	S	■	S	E	A	T
S	E	M	I	■	O	T	B	■	H	U	R	T	S	■
■	■	■	V	I	C	H	Y	S	S	O	I	S	E	■
■	G	H	E	T	T	O	B	L	A	S	T	E	R	■
■	L	E	B	R	O	N	J	A	M	E	S	■	■	■
F	O	R	A	Y	■	O	M	S	■	M	A	S	K	■
U	B	E	R	■	P	E	R	P	■	L	E	T	H	E
T	U	G	■	B	A	G	N	O	L	D	■	T	O	N
I	L	O	V	E	L	A	■	E	S	O	T	E	R	Y
L	I	E	A	B	E	D	■	T	A	P	I	N	T	O
E	N	S	L	E	R	■	S	T	A	N	D	I	N	■

41

J	E	D	I	M	A	S	T	E	R	■	S	P	A	M
A	L	O	H	A	S	T	A	T	E	■	N	O	N	E
M	I	R	A	C	L	E	M	A	X	■	A	L	A	N
E	X	I	T	■	A	P	P	S	■	P	A	C	S	■
S	I	T	E	■	N	S	A	■	I	N	A	R	O	W
■	R	O	I	L	■	■	A	C	E	T	O	N	E	■
■	■	T	O	Y	B	O	X	E	S	■	I	D	A	■
A	S	H	■	G	O	A	L	I	E	S	■	D	A	R
U	T	A	■	J	U	R	A	S	S	I	C	■	■	■
D	E	N	M	A	R	K	■	■	E	A	R	L	■	■
I	M	G	A	M	E	■	S	M	U	■	S	E	E	S
E	W	O	K	■	■	O	T	O	S	■	E	V	A	N
N	A	V	E	■	C	H	O	R	U	S	L	I	N	E
C	R	E	D	■	D	O	M	E	A	F	A	V	O	R
E	E	R	O	■	S	H	A	L	L	O	W	E	N	D

42

I	N	S	■	R	I	B	S	■	■	D	I	C	E	Y
D	O	T	H	E	M	A	T	H	■	A	D	O	R	E
I	F	E	E	L	F	R	E	E	■	F	I	L	E	S
D	A	I	R	Y	■	G	E	M	■	T	O	D	A	Y
S	I	N	E	■	G	A	R	I	■	■	T	O	D	O
O	R	S	■	A	R	I	■	N	Y	U	■	P	E	U
■	■	■	T	R	A	N	S	G	E	N	D	E	R	■
■	■	A	I	N	T	I	A	W	O	M	A	N	■	■
■	■	D	O	M	A	I	N	N	A	M	E	S	■	■
L	O	L	■	Z	A	G	■	Y	E	T	■	G	I	G
A	G	R	A	■	C	O	E	N	■	M	O	N	O	■
S	P	A	S	M	■	H	R	S	■	B	A	N	J	O
H	A	D	T	O	■	I	N	Q	U	I	R	E	O	F
E	R	I	E	S	■	P	O	U	N	D	C	A	K	E
S	K	O	R	T	■	T	E	E	S	■	R	E	D	■

43

```
M E A S U R I N G S T I C K S
I A P P R E C I A T E T H A T
S T R A I T O F M E S S I N A
H O O T S   S T E A L   L E X
A N N     S A Y     M A D D  
      N A E             O B I
T O T A L I T A R I A N I S M
I C O U L D E A T A H O R S E
P U R S U E T H E M A T T E R
S L E E P L E S S N I G H T S
    I T A         O R O      
    O M A N   T E T     A S S
A P B   W O M E N   P I L O T
L A I D I T O N T H E L I N E
I N T E R E S T R A T E C A P
T E S T E D T H E W A T E R S
```

44

```
  S A M O A N     A R M P I T
W H O A W H O A   D I V I D E
H A R D S E L L   R E P A I D
O N T     M O L T E N   N O T
L I A M     S H I P   B O L A
L A S E R B E A M   R E B E L
      R I O   L I F E H A C K
  L O R D V O L D E M O R T  
L E F I G A R O   N I L      
E M C E E   I W O N T D O I T
N O O R   L O S T     S Y N E
G N U   M I N E T A     S T E
T O R T E S   V E R B O T E N
H I S S A T   E R E A D E R S
S L E E T S     S A Y E R S  
```

45

```
S H A R D   A N T E   S T O P
W E B E R   M A R I J U A N A
I R O N Y   I C E L A N D I C
M O V E R   C H E A P D A T E
    E G O B O O S T E R      
    S W E A R       D E B T S
P T A   S O U P U P   S L O P
H O T S T O N E M A S S A G E
D U E T   M C C A I N   C A D
S T R O P         N O O K S  
    W O W J U S T W O W      
A S K A N Y O N E   C L I F F
S L O W D A N C E   R A D I O
T U N A S T E A K   A L O N G
I G G Y   T S P S   B A W D Y
```

46

```
N E W T   A F L A C   T Y K E
O V E R   R O A C H   H O A X
S I L O   A G R E E   Y U R I
E L L I E   L A T E   L A S  
J E S S E J A M E S   M O O T
O S H   G U M   N E W C O K E
B T U S   S P F   P A R K E D
    T H A T S A B I G I F    
A L M O N D   B O Z   B A S H
C O Y O T E S   O Z S   M O O
D A M S   S C A M A R T I S T
E N O   E L E M   S A L U T  
L O U D   R E G I S   L I E U
C U T E   T R I C K   I A M B
O T H O   S A S S Y   A R E S
```

47

```
S N A P C H A T   C L A S S Y
K E T E L O N E   H A L I T E
I C E R I N K S   A N I M A L
    S M E L T R O E   O I L  
C A N O E   E R O S   E N D S
A N O N   S M U G   M A C    
C G I   S T O N E M A S O N S
H E S S I A N   R E N E W A L
E L E C T R I C F A N   E V E
    M A Z   T H E N   C L A W
H E A T   V O I D   R O L L S
E L K   C O R D E L I A      
L I E L O W   I R O N C H E F
E T R A D E   N E W S H O L E
N E S T E D   G R E E K G O D
```

48

```
D A R K A N G E L   T R A P  
I N A C L A I R E   C H E M O
K I M J O N G U N   H E R B S
  S I O N   A D D T O C A R T
P E N N E   H I L O   A T O I
B E T E   S E T   U N R E S T
A D O S   T R E S P A S S E S
      A R T   Y E P        
G Q M A G A Z I N E   L A P S
S U I T E S   N T S   O D I N
T E S T   S A S H   I C A L L
R E S I D E N C E   M A W S  
I N U R E   D A T A P L A N S
N I S E I   O L I V E T R E E
G E A R   R E C E I V E R S  
```

49

S	E	A	L	E	D	W	I	T	H	A	K	I	S	S
A	L	L	O	V	E	R	T	H	E	P	L	A	C	E
B	A	G	G	A	G	E	C	A	R	O	U	S	E	L
A	N	I	O	N	■	S	A	T	E	S	■	S	P	F
D	T	E	N	■	A	T	M	O	S	■	K	U	T	I
O	R	R	■	H	E	L	E	N	■	A	I	M	E	E
■	A	S	H	O	R	E	■	E	A	R	N	E	R	■
■	■	A	M	I	■	■	C	U	D	■	■	■	■	■
■	M	O	N	I	E	S	■	H	U	M	A	N	E	■
B	I	N	G	E	■	T	T	O	P	S	■	A	L	P
I	L	L	S	■	B	E	A	T	S	■	G	I	N	A
S	E	E	■	I	R	A	N	I	■	S	A	V	O	R
T	R	A	C	T	O	R	T	R	A	I	L	E	R	S
R	U	S	S	I	A	N	R	O	U	L	E	T	T	E
O	N	H	A	N	D	S	A	N	D	K	N	E	E	S

50

T	A	P	S	■	C	L	A	P	■	T	O	N	G	A
O	B	O	E	■	H	E	A	L	T	H	F	O	O	D
Y	O	K	E	■	I	N	R	A	R	E	F	O	R	M
S	U	E	S	■	S	T	O	N	E	H	E	N	G	E
■	T	R	A	D	E	O	N	■	V	E	R	E	E	N
B	A	G	F	U	L	■	■	K	I	A	■	■	■	■
A	B	A	T	E	■	■	S	A	I	N	T	H	O	O	D
R	O	M	E	■	G	O	T	T	O	■	O	R	Z	O
E	V	E	R	H	Y	M	E	S	■	A	R	G	O	N
■	■	■	A	P	E	■	■	I	N	S	A	N	E	■
A	T	B	A	T	S	■	P	A	N	T	E	N	E	■
B	Y	A	C	C	I	D	E	N	T	■	H	I	H	O
U	P	S	T	H	E	A	N	T	E	■	I	Z	O	D
Z	E	R	O	E	S	I	N	O	N	■	D	E	L	I
Z	B	A	R	S	■	S	E	N	D	■	E	D	E	N

The New York Times

Crossword Puzzles

The #1 Name in Crosswords

Available at your local bookstore or online at nytimes.com/nytstore

St. Martin's Griffin